The Lion in the Park

The Lion in the Park

The Life and Works of Blanche Nevin

Biography and poetry of Blanche Nevin
the sculptress and world traveler
1841-1925

Churchtown, Pennsylvania

by
Phyllis Jean Smith Brubaker
1997

Rutledge Books, Inc.

Bethel, CT

Rutledge Books, Inc.
8 F.J. Clarke Circle, Bethel, CT 06801

Manufactured in the United States of America

Cataloging in Publication Data
Brubaker, Phyllis Jean Smith.
   The lion in the park : the life and works of
Blanche Nevin /
by Phyllis Jean Smith Brubaker.
      p. cm.
   ISBN 1-887750-44-4
   1. Nevin, Blanche. 2. Sculptors--United States--
Biography. I. Title.
730.92--dc20   LC 96-71050
[B]   CIP

Dedication

This book is dedicated to my family and friends who have given my life purpose and pleasure.

—Phyllis Jean Smith Brubaker
1997

Contents

This was the moment of international acclaim for Blanche Nevin, yet her name was misspelled. Cinderella is sitting reading an invitation, and Eve is standing nude shielding her eyes. Blanche's marble of Maud Muller was in the Hall of Honor at the Chicago International Exposition in 1879.

Preface

Altoona Tribune, 1913

"Pennsylvania overlooks the fame of its native artists and sculptors and shows encouragement to many less gifted who come from a distance. While Blanche Nevin, America's foremost sculpture and resident of Lancaster County, has been signally honored, yet there are many of us who are not aware of the magnitude of her talents.

Ever since she scored her great triumph in having her statue of General Muhlenberg placed in Statuary Hall in the national Capitol, her place in the artistic world has been secure. This statue is held by many to be the most finished piece in the collection, which included examples by most of the foremost sculptors. Foreigners have been particularly impressed by it, especially those with discriminating tastes.

*It is a pity, however, that more of Miss Nevin's works do not adorn public places. Her bust of Woodrow Wilson, made at the beginning of the late campaign, was considered the official likeness of the popular candidate. Many replicas were made and it enjoyed widespread popularity. The **Tribune** hopes that someday a copy will be cut in marble and placed at the Capitol in Harrisburg. It would serve as an inspiration to young Pennsylvania sculptors, causing them to realize that there is a field for them where their talents will be properly recognized."*

Author's Note:

The preceding article explains my most important reason for writing a biography of Blanche Nevin's life. The prevailing view seems to be that sculpture doesn't fit a fine art definition. It seems to me that sculpture involves a higher degree of talent in thinking abstractly as well as the talent that becomes the skill with hammer and chisel.

Blanche Nevin did not have access to electrical saws and cutters that are used in 1996 to more quickly complete a piece. Blanche studied the use of stone cutting chisels and rasps, to work the stone with masters of the art at home and abroad.

Her poetry was a creative use of everyday items that provoked certain feelings and thoughts that she wrote in verse. Sometimes she lapsed into the flowery and esoteric verbiage as in the lengthy poem she wrote and read at the George Ross historic marker dedication. This was the custom of her time.

Acknowledgements

I have enjoyed the search for facts as recorded over many years by many people about Blanche Nevin. Some sources simply verified data from another source.

The help of these persons greatly facilitated my search. My sincere thank you to the librarians and archivists. Many of the museums in Philadelphia responded with or without materials. Some called to hear more of what I had found. I am grateful for all the people with a sense of history. The following persons were especially knowledgeable and helpful:

Leo Shelley, Millersville University, Ganser Library

Jon Weaver Kreider, Librarian, Mennonite Historical Society

Philip Metzger, Lehigh University, Bethlehem, PA

Tom Collins, Proprietor, Sayre Mansion Inn, Bethlehem, PA

Historic Preservation Trust, Lancaster, PA

Kevin Shue, Search Coordinator, Lancaster County Historical Society

Lance Metz, Historian, Hugh Moore Park and Canal Museum, Easton, PA

Jerald Martin, President of Churchtown Historical Society, Churchtown, PA

Steve L. Zerbe, Research Archivist, The Civil War Library and Museum, Philadelphia, PA

Marietta Boyer, Archivist, Pennsylvania Academy of Fine Arts, Philadelphia

Anne Kenne and Andrew Gulati, Librarians, Fackenthal Library, Franklin and Marshall College

Virginia Smith, Historian Associate, Mercersburg Historical Society and Kittochtinny Historians

Historical Society, Chambersburg, PA

George M. White, FAIA, Architect of the Capitol, Washington, DC

John W. W. Loose, Historian, Past President, Lancaster County Historical Society

James L. Stokes, Research Assistant, Lancaster County Historical Society

Theresa Snyder, Assistant Director, The University Archives and Records Center, University of Pennsylvania

Carol Faill, Rothman Gallery, Franklin and Marshall College

Rev. John Weiler, Bethlehem

Rev. Amos Seldomridge, Woxall

Diane Russell, Researcher, Evangelical Reformed Historical Society

Helen Hager, Source on provenance marble bust at Iris Club

Faith Sayre Schindler, Grandniece of Blanche

Richard Hertzler, Photographer for Blanche self portrait reproduction

Alvin Weaver, Personal acquaintance, Century-old interviewee

And most especially a grateful thank you to my typist and computer operator, *Erika Flood*, of Dedicated Office Services. I found her to be enthusiastic about the project as a valuable biography on our Lancaster County artist.

Foreword

Several years ago, Phyllis Brubaker, member of the Iris Club and Chair of the Fine Arts Committee, became interested in writing a book about Blanche Nevin. Blanche, a cosmopolitan woman and a leader in the arts, was Pennsylvania's foremost sculptress in her day.

Well known as a sculptress, artist, and poetess, Blanche was also a world traveler with influence that expanded from her beloved restored home, Windsor Mansion, in Churchtown, Pennsylvania, to Lancaster and Washington, DC. Her greatest triumph is the statue of General Muhlenberg, which stands in Statuary Hall in the National Capitol Building in Washington.

Blanche is also known for the bust of President Woodrow Wilson and, locally, for the beautiful fountain which she presented to the City of Lancaster, her home from age 14 to 21 years of age. This spectacular example of her skill features a bronze reclining lion, and lends its title to that of this book: *Lion in the Park*.

In Brubaker's narrative we learn that Blanche and her sister, Alice, founder of the Iris Club, were women with leadership qualities and original thinkers who lent their spirit to community activities.

If genius, or the studious brain
By happy chance, should kindly deign
To tap upon thy wooden side
Open my door, fly open wide.

Blanche Nevin, **To My Door**

Jerald Martin
Caernarvon Township
Churchtown, PA
June 1996

Introduction

The preceding article as *Preface* explains one reason for a biography of Blanche Nevin's life. It still seems that sculpture, especially by a woman of the Victorian times, does not fit many persons' definition of womanly activity.

The difficulties of painting and sculpture are really not comparable, as sculpture requires a degree of abstraction and imagination that does not rely upon color as stimulus. Both art forms come from talent and skill, but appear in different images.

Reaching the age of 81, Blanche Nevin painted a very good self-portrait and recorded it by having her picture taken with the portrait. She was working on a model of "Peace," at her death, a sculpture she had wished to give to the nation. Its location is unknown. We know more about Blanche's pieces of sculpture than her paintings. It seems that she preferred to study sculpture and did so in several countries. Too many of her sculptures seem lost, but the names and descriptions will be included with the several that have been located.

Blanche was noted by many writers of annals of local history, but there has been some misinformation that will be corrected in this biography. Pieces of her poems were printed, however, this search has found 50 complete poems included in the poetry chapter.

Believing that the family history was important, it was with delight that I read Blanche's own family history that she wrote for a visit to Windsor Forge by the Berks County Historical Society. The biography will end with Blanche's own writing, (1921), at 80 years of age.

Blanche's life was of the same era of artistic growth as Lloyd Mifflin and Charles Demuth. Perhaps in her patriarchal family only poetry and intellectual, theological pursuits were deemed worthy of notice.

With her honorary sculptures for her parents, she succeeded in not sinking into oblivion although she was a woman, and proved her talent for all to see, with her lasting gifts to her parents and the city of Lancaster. This biography will add more to our knowledge of Blanche, her life, and her considerable talent.

When the author first heard of Blanche and Windsor Forge in 1956, it did not leave her memory. Over the years it seemed that so little of her life was known by Lancastrians, so in 1993, the search began in earnest. But because of the lost sculptures, there is still a feeling of missing information. Perhaps someone else will find them, or this book will bring them into public knowledge.

One

Who Was Blanche Nevin?

Having been told of Blanche Nevin in about 1955 by Jean Seldomridge, wife of the Reverend Amos Seldomridge, our family drove to Churchtown to see Windsor Forge. It had become quite overgrown with brush in the terraced area at the rear; in fact, there were cattle grazing very near the mansion, and there is no memory of a fence. The terraces were disappearing. We peeped in windows and saw the bust draped, sitting on what seemed to be a grand piano. That draped bust, according to the story, was President Wilson. Blanche did not approve of his League of Nations activity during his Presidency. At that time, it seemed to add to the understanding of Blanche and her political views that were probably formed as a result of time abroad, and her strong character. Whether President Wilson's remarriage to someone else had any bearing on her views is not known.

The more that was learned of Blanche, as the research began in earnest three years ago, the more appropriate it seemed to apply family constellation theory. The hypothesis was formed that Blanche was a middle child in the birth order of her siblings.

You will see in the second chapter, that Blanche was the fourth birth in a series of eight births, proving the hypothesis. It can be conjectured that there were contributing factors to her development from the information that her elder sister, Alice Nevin, walked all her life with a severe limp. Additionally, Blanche was born the same year that her infant third brother died. So, as Blanche was born in Mercersburg, her parents were grieving. She was an adolescent when they moved to the rural setting of Windsor Hall for two years while Caernarvon Place

1

was being built on Columbia Avenue in Lancaster. It has been found, using the date of her father's letter in the Appendix, that she went to Philadelphia to live and study at age 21.

Miss Stahr wrote that Blanche was always creating fun and had a very pleasant personality, while Alice, her older sister, was more sober and not as sociable.[25, Vol. 75]

Some have said that Blanche was not involved with her family. This does not appear to be true, as research of her brother-in-law's diary has shown. Fortunately, he wrote of family matters as well as references to Andrew Carnegie.[9] Blanche's younger sister Martha, nicknamed Patty, married and lived in Bethlehem. Blanche visited frequently in Bethlehem, and Patty and her two sons spent time at the shore with Blanche. Without access to Blanche's incidental writing or records, this book will be the most information about Blanche in one place. It does, by necessity, include other appropriate bits of history occurring during her 84-year life span.

At the beginning of the research, there was little appreciation of the influence the whole Nevin family maintained wherever they lived. An interesting side issue was the diverse religious denominations represented within the three generations: Presbyterian, Episcopal, Protestant Episcopal, and Evangelical United Church.[5,36]

Nothing explicit about Blanche's religious convictions, but by her nature it would be doubtful if it was the same as her parents. However, the Buddha Ghatama sculpture on her front lawn indicated that she looked into the Eastern religions while traveling in China and Japan. She did internalize the quietness inherent in the yoga, and sculpted the Buddha as an art exercise rather than a matter of worship. Her father also had a keen interest in Oriental culture.

Another area of interest which arose was the individuality among the Nevin children. The Reverend John Williamson Nevin himself was well aware of "The Ethical Culture Movement" of the 1870s founded by Felix Adler. "The movement attracted people who were distressed by the condition of an increasingly urban and industrial society and who no longer found the tenets of traditional religion acceptable. In essence a religion of morality, looking for true simplicity in living and sincere purity in morals and manners."[11]

Education became its main agent. Several schools were sponsored, including the first kindergarten in Lancaster and on the entire east coast. It was sponsored by Alice Nevin—tuition free—in her home. Some of the extinct county and city schools were found as the author tried to find how the girls in the Nevin family were educated. In the Lampeter-Strasburg district there were Bunker Hill (1885); Lyndon School, Lyndon, at Eckman Road (1875); Maple Craft School at Penn Grant Road and Beaver Valley (1906); and North Jackson Street School, Strasburg (1808). In Lancaster City there were Miss Stahr's School (1901); Irving College for Young Women, Female High School (1862); Seminary for Young Ladies (1865); and Conestoga Collegiate Institute (1865), located at 325 S. Lime Street. Linden Hall was founded in 1746 in Lititz; Simpson/Lauver Young Women's Academy in Marietta; Windsor Female Academy at Windsor Mansion (1867), was taught by Blanche's Aunt Phoebe, Mrs. P. A. Scott, and daughters. This school held classes in English Branches, Latin, French, History, Natural Science, Mathematics, and Mental and Moral Philosophy. There were two sessions with two quarters each session; Lancaster College (1906-1908) was formerly called Madame Cotta College until it merged with Miss Stahr's school to form the Shippen School.[24,25,Vol.29,38,39] The latter were the nucleus of the Lancaster Country Day School.

It was finally found that the Nevin girls were tutored at home by the most highly educated teachers the Nevins could hire. The sons went off to college, as was typical of those times. The schools were "developed to combine industrial and cultural education to prepare students for their future station in life but also make them capable of living in a truly human way. Dignity and worth of the individual and the value of art and science to the elevation of man's nature and moral superiority of the simple life style."[11]

This Ethical Culture thinking seems to have been the progenitor of the Nevin off-springs' strivings as they led their diverse lives, all managing to contribute to society in their own way.

Because of the time in history, Blanche seems the most individualistic of all the Nevins, as she sought the experiences that helped her gain some satisfaction, as a woman, in those Victorian times.

The creative approach to her activities, along with her generalist learnings, allowed her to branch out in several directions, spending major time with the cultural arts. It affected the eclectic choice of her imported furniture and paintings. It was visible in her restoration of Windsor Hall to Windsor Forge to honor the Forge ancestors.

In the Lancaster County Historical Society file on Blanche, there are several newspaper pictures of her home during the 28 years she lived back in Lancaster County. Some of her furniture, as well as the interior and exterior, have been photograped, to be included in a later chapter.

In 1915, Blanche's home was described as a historic and romantic Italian villa with tall oak, maple, and walnut trees and vines of every description. And the huge clay lion (model for the bronze one in Reservoir Park) on the front lawn was such that "when a visitor approaches he expects to hear a roar."[25, Vol. 19]

The influences of Blanche's travels are visible, and her little studio at the back of the house was where she sculpted her smaller pieces. She finished the Muhlenberg statue at Windsor after beginning it in Carrara, Italy.[11]

Blanche's sense of the "country estate" helped her envision the finished restoration and additions. There were three terraces down the slope in the back lawn toward the "soggy" bottom, now a farm-type pond that the spring in back of the mansion drains into before emptying into the head waters of the Conestoga River, which begins about one mile east toward Morgantown.

The restoration spanned a busy one-and-one-half years. Several local men who had the necessary skills found work at Windsor Forge. Among them Robert Simpson, later a teacher and *The Rambler* essayist.

The pergola of columns extended some 20 to 60 feet from the

end of the house parallel with Windsor Road. Covered with vines, it provided privacy on the side lawn and was a shady promenade.

Blanche has been credited with adding the diamond paned windows that enhance the beautiful front entrance which create the Italianate Villa visage.

With twelve owners, the old mansion seems to have had two major restorations and improvements. For future historians the list of owners follows as found:

1. David Jenkins immigrated from Wales in the 1730s and settled in Chester County;

2. John Jenkins received the land grant from William Penn of 400 acres in Caernarvon Township;

3. He sold it to William Branson, Philadelphia, who was scouting for iron rich land. After building five forges and the original part of the mansion he sold it to his employee, the second David Jenkins, son of John, making David the third owner;

4. Robert Jenkins, grandson of John Jenkins;

5. David Jenkins, son of Robert, was Blanche's uncle;

6. At David's death it reverted to his mother, Catherine Carmichael Jenkins;

7. Elizabeth Jenkins Reigart was Blanche's aunt;

8. Catherine Reigart Cummins, daughter of Elizabeth, sold it to her cousin;

9. Blanche Nevin, granddaughter of Catherine Jenkins, for $18,000 with 26 acres or 34 acres;

10. Reverend John Nevin Sayre, Blanche's nephew inherited; and

11. Mrs. Roland Brown, a grandniece in Ohio, now owns it under the National Register of Historic Places and the Lancaster Historic Preservation Trust Survey of places to be preserved. Carol and George Lux leased it with intent to buy. George died and Carol and her son still live there in 1995.

The current residents have done much restoration inside and out and have modernized within the Preservation guidelines. This may be tedious reading, but it invokes the names of many well-known figures in past Lancaster County history.

There are no longer visible traces of the housing for the 38 slaves the Jenkins held at one time. Some came with the property when purchased from Branson and Lardner, Branson's son-in-law partner.

The Civil War was accepted by the John Nevin family with the two eldest sons going to war, both becoming captains. How the Jenkins side of the family felt is not clear, but according to the plan said to be used to free slaves, the Emancipation Proclamation would have freed their slaves much earlier. The Jenkins' plan was used by many owners. The first slave they bought was theirs for his entire life, his children were slaves to a certain age, usually early sixties, and then freed, and then that slaves' children were born free. It took three generations to be free under this widely used plan.

The forges were getting past their peak with steel and iron products being produced in the growing industrialization of manufacturing. So the slaves were not needed for forge work even if there had not been a Civil War. Many of the slaves of that region moved on to the Welsh Mountains and stayed in the locality, finding work as they could.[12]

The premise that Blanche seemed unknown did not hold up as she was listed in many dictionaries devoted to American artists and sculptors. She is listed in both Philadelphia and Chicago Exposition histories as an exhibitor and 16 volumes of Lancaster County Historical Society minutes record some of her activities in their organization since it's first year. The "Souvenir of the Pilgrimage of the Historical Society of Berks County to Windsor Forges, 1742, Caernarvon Township, Lancaster, Pennsylvania, September 2, 1921" written by Blanche Nevin will be included in its entirety because it is her history and genealogical writing of her ancestry and home.

Six biographical annals of Lancaster County (surprise! there are more than one in print, but not all are of the same time period) mentioned Blanche in some form. Her family constellation and history will follow in chapter two.

The J. W. Nevin family helped found Clio—the Cliosophic Society—and this group still holds its meetings at the Iris Club in

Lancaster. The first meetings were held in members' homes until the group outgrew the homes. The Clio was a group for people who like to examine topics, sometimes studying one topic the whole season. Its evolution has brought it to listening to speakers with some discussion following, and traditionally ice cream has always been the refreshment.

James Buchanan was a personal friend of the Nevin family, living just across the field from Caernarvon Place on Columbia Avenue at President Avenue. The Degel Israel Synagogue now stands on the site. The carriage house still stands behind the synagogue. Mrs. Nevin wrote a lengthy thank you to President Buchanan for the invitation to his inaugural ceremony. Her remarks about the severe cold verifies other historic accounts of his inauguration. Another note told of her gratitude for Miss Hettie's assistance. Miss Hettie was Buchanan's housekeeper.[36] Blanche is thought to be the artist of the Harriet Lane portrait hanging in the Iris Club. The name has been badly scratched, but "B/L" does appear in the first name, and the Nevin is more clear. There are no records found in this research of Alice or Patty Nevin being painters.

Blanche and the other Nevin women could have been members of the Daughters of the Revolution because five of the Jenkins ancestors' graves have the 1776 marker, all in a row, in Old Bangor Cemetery in Churchtown.

During her time at Windsor Forge after the Civil War, Blanche held a picnic each year on May 30 for Civil War veterans on her back lawn, utilizing her huge stone table, which is told about in a later chapter.[12]

There is little information about Blanche before she left home to study in Philadelphia. Contrary to some records she did not appear on any class lists at the Pennsylvania Academy of Fine Art, but did exhibit in their shows of 1876-1913. Her address was 1022 Market Street, Philadelphia. There will be more about her work for the show in the chapter listing her sculptures.

Blanche wrote many poems and set some to music. She would sing them accompanying herself on her guitar. Her living room was graced by a grand piano, and by all indications, Blanche and her sisters all played piano, as did their mother, Martha Jenkins Nevin.

Blanche does not appear on the Iris Club membership lists, but she was a member of The Lancaster County Historical Society from its first year and held membership in the Numismatic Club in New York and The Geographical Society there also.

Patty, (Martha), the youngest sister, did marry well even though her husband was many years her senior. Robert Sayre was the chief engineer and general supervisor of the Lehigh Valley Railroad. He had a very large part in the design and building of the Railroad from 1852-1899. For three years he was a board member of the unsuccessful Southern Penn Railroad. The Southern Penn right-of-way was later used, when feasible, for the Pennsylvania Turnpike design. He owned a bank, a hotel in Bethlehem, and the iron and steel mill that designed and made the first iron ships used in Civil War battles.[9] The ships were called Monitors, and eventually the Southern Confederacy was also using iron ships.[54] Sayre also had conversations with Andrew Carnegie concerning steel production, as noted in his diaries.

Mr. Sayre kept diaries during his 25-year marriage to Patty. Fortunately, he recorded family happenings as well as meetings with Andrew Carnegie and Asa Packer. Blanche's many visits were noted in the diaries, and bits of her history and involvement with her family were affirmed. At 38, studying sculpture and art in Philadelphia and Italy, Blanche continued to travel to warmer climates for most winters. She made at least five trips to Italy, according to the writings of *The Rambler*, Robert Simpson Caernarvon Township, Churchtown, PA. Mr. Simpson had worked summers for Blanche as a young man. There will be more about him in the anecdotal section.

Blanche wrote a genealogical history for the Berks County Historical Society visit that provides, in her words, how the siblings were influential in many areas around the world. Martha (Patty) Jenkins, the youngest sister of Blanche, was the only one of the five Nevin offspring to marry. Her husband, Robert Sayre of Bethlehem, had been married and widowed three times with seven children when he and Patty married. Robert and Patty had two sons who had a priv-ileged life, with private schooling at Belmont School and Ivy league degrees.[8] John Nevin Sayre, a Reverend Doctor, was known for his activity in the Foundation of Reconciliation, acting as its President. He was with Blanche when she died and inherited Windsor Forge. In about 1929-30, Sayre offered Blanche's historic home, with all fur-nishings, to the State of Pennsylvania as a house museum. It was refused, and the property was rented for many years. In 1937, John Sayre and his wife brought their two daughters, Faith and Heather, to visit Mrs. Minnie Davis, who occupied Windsor for many years. The last address found for him was Ferris Lane, Nyack, New York. He had served as pastor of a small Episcopal Church in Suffern, New York, during World War I. Francis Bowes Sayre, "Frank" to his family[8], was introduced to Jessie Wilson, daughter of Woodrow Wilson, by Aunt Blanche when she invited Jessie to come to Windsor while Frank was on Easter recess from Princeton. Blanche seized the opportunity to write a poem and sang it to Jessie as she entered the lovely front door. The young couple took walks and went on picnics, going into Lancaster to see Wild Bill Cody Wild West Show. After an engagement of three years, and after Wilson was elected President, the couple was married in the East Room of the White House. It was reported that Aunt Blanche, sitting near the front during the ceremony in a violent purple dress, with her many bracelets that she always wore, broke the silence with their jangling. Frank and Jessie's first and second child were born in the White House.

The young couple, with a young baby were called to Siam (Thailand) for Francis to aid in opening trade with the world—truly opening Siam to the world. They then were sent to the Phillipines for Francis to serve as High Commissioner of the territory.* He was called from his next position as Director of the New York Penal System by President Franklin Roosevelt to the post of Assistant Secretary of State. It was he who carried the note to the Japanese Ambassador to tell Japan that we were cutting off all trade in early October 1941. This was one of two precipitating actions that may have forced the Japanese to attack Pearl Harbor. This delivery was in early October, after a notification during the summer before that the US was suspending all talks. Later in November, a message may have been intercepted by the Japanese that 25,000 more troops were on their way to the Pacific. The troops had not arrived when the bombing of Pearl Harbor occurred. The War Department sent a message that there was danger of an imminent bombing, but, to avoid detection it was sent by regular mail and did not arrive before the catastrophe of Pearl Harbor. There has been nothing found that President Franklin Roosevelt knew of any warnings of the attack. Both sides underestimated the others' strength.[55]

Blanche did not live to see how important her nephews became.

---

*Author's note: Faith Sayre Schindler, niece of Francis, gave the information that at the time of Pearl Harbor, Francis Sayre's family escaped to Correigidor and was then rescued and returned to the States by submarine.

Two

Blanche's Family Life

Martha Jenkins Nevin, Blanche's mother, was personally refined, well versed in literature and could write for the press when the occasion called for it. She devoted herself to her family and drew around her people of cultivation and superior social standing. She was born on July 4, 1805, and died January 13, 1890. She was a widow for four years.[11]

Martha Jenkins Nevin was the daughter of Robert Jenkins and Catherine Mustard Carmichael Jenkins. Robert Jenkins was ironmaster for five forges, and served Lancaster County in the State Legislature (1807-1811). He served two terms in Congress during which time the family lived in Washington, DC. Robert was a stern, inflexible patriot. He was the great-grandson of David Jenkins who came from Wales and settled in Chester County before it became a part of Lancaster County in 1729.

The original land grant from Penn was for 400 acres along the Conestoga Creek. After meandering past Brownstown, it becomes the Conestoga River around Lancaster, and empties into the Susquehanna at Safe Harbor, P.A.[12]

John Jenkins' (son of David Jenkins) family lived in caves at first, before the small out-building to the right of the mansion was built. Branson is credited with building the old part of the mansion while Robert built the larger addition to accommodate his family of seven. The old part was built in 1743.[12]

"In 1768, December 28, in Hartford, Connecticut, The Susquehanna Company availed itself of the withdrawal of the

Indians, voted that forty persons upwards of twenty-one years of age, proprietors in the purchase and approved by commissioners, proceed to take possession by the 1st of February...200£ be appropriated for materials and provisions for said forty; that five townships be laid out each five miles square, three on one side of the river and two on the other of the Susquehanna River, the forty persons first coming to choose a township, which should be divided among them in addition to their shares, three shares in each township to be set apart for a Gospel minister and schools, the grant of the holdings to be conditioned upon occupation and improvement in five years, and upon good behavior, and of not holding any part of the company's land under pretense of any other title than the company's. All iron and coal were reserved for after disposal. Isaac Tripp, Benjamin Follett, John Jenkins, William Buck, and Benjamin Shoemaker were to superintend the affairs of the forty, first coming, including laying out of a road to the Susquehanna River; and upon the arrival of the whole two hundred persons, might increase this latter committee to nine, who would then regulate the affairs of the settlers until further order..."[54] John Jenkins was Blanche's great grandfather who received and sold the original grant at Windsor.

This writing shows how Blanche's ancestor was involved in the very beginning of the county. This all occurred after many years of dealing with Indian tribes to secure their land. Wampum belts were passed, but whether payments were accurate it does not say. Also, the source book had Nathan Schaeffer, Ph.D. as one of the authors.

It is interesting that John Jenkins sold his rich land after nine years to Branson and Lardner for their forges. John's son David worked in the forges' office and then bought them out. The Jenkins' wealth grew during the Revolutionary War and after the estate grew to 3,000 acres. John is one of the 1776 men in Old Bangor grave yard.

Blanche's grandmother, Catherine C. Jenkins, used land on top of the Churchtown Hill and had a fieldstone church built in 1850 where the Jenkins family worshipped as Presbyterians. The later generations of Jenkins are buried beside Catherine's church. The John W. Nevins family is buried in Woodward Hill Cemetery in Lancaster. The William Jenkins and Alfred Nevin burials were in Lancaster Cemetery.

The Jenkins-Carmichael marriage was blessed with five daughters and two sons. Blanche's maternal aunts and uncles were Elizabeth, wife of Philip Wagner Reigart; Phoebe Ann, wife of the Reverend John W. Scott, president of Washington and Jefferson College; Catherine, wife of General Hanson Bentley Jacobs of Churchtown; Mary, wife of the Reverend William W. Latta, pastor of Honeybrook Church; Sarah, wife of the Reverend Alfred Nevin, D.D. Presbyterian minister and brother of J. W. Nevin; Martha, married to the Reverend John Williamson Nevin, second president of Franklin and Marshall College; and Dr. John Carmichael Jenkins, who inherited the Carmichael estate in Mississippi, where he left a large family. He was a doctor during a typhoid epidemic and died himself. David Jenkins built the Twin Linden Mansion (now a bed and breakfast inn) and was the last forge master. At his death, the forge reverted back to his mother Catherine. By that time the forge era was waning due to industrialization and new methods.[12, 6, 7] It was operated a few years by others.[12, 6, 7]

On Blanche's paternal side, the Reverend Dr. J. W. Nevin was born in northern Franklin County and came to Lancaster County as a youth when his father moved to the Lampeter-Strasburg area to farm. There were six sons and three daughters in that family. Most of the sons went to Union College and later to Princeton University to complete their education. J. W. Nevin, Blanche's father, went to Union College and to Princeton University for his seminary training. After his three years as a student, he was asked to teach for three years in the Seminary to fill a temporary vacancy. At the end of that term, he went to the Allegheny Western Seminary to teach near Pittsburgh. He and Martha Jenkins were married in 1835. The marriage was solemnized by The Rev. John Wallace, Presbyterian minister of Pequea, on New Year's Day.

J. W. is reported to have lived with another minister's family for three years while at Allegheny Seminary before his marriage. Three

13

children were born during his ten-year tenure in Western Seminary. In 1840, he was brought to Mercersburg Seminary. He was 40 years old when he began that twelve-year tenure. During this time he wrote *The Mystical Presence* and saw the birth of an infant son in 1840, who died before Blanche was born, in 1841. The work that made J.W. important in the reform movement was *The Mercersburg Theology,* a theology of the New Testament. He succeeded Dr. Rauch as head of the Mercersburg seminary.[2, 9]

"The Reverend Doctor Nevin felt no pride in maintaining an unvarying uniformity of thought. Single facts possessed value for him only as they were comprehended in a general life. His mind was always open in a childlike way to influence of other strong minds, but it was too vigorous and healthy to succumb to them in absolute submission".[11]

His brother, Rev. Alfred said of Rev. John, "in the domestic circle he was thought affable and kind, generally dignified and silent in manner".[11]

Blanche was twelve when they left Linden Avenue in Mercersburg to live for two years in Windsor Forge, while the new mansion on Columbia Avenue in Lancaster was being built. The Nevins settled Catherine's estate after her death and buried her in the church yard by the Presbyterian Church that was used only a few years. It is now under Historic Preservation and houses the Churchtown Historical Society archives. In 1876, the Nevin family moved to Caernarvon Place in Lancaster and continued a friendship with their neighbor, James Buchanan. J. W. was made president of the new Franklin and Marshall College, following a term (1841-1853) as president of Marshall College in Mercersburg and then the term from 1866 to 1876 at F & M College. J. W. died in his 84th year (1803-1886), in his beloved Caernarvon Place. He had officiated at his friend Buchanan's burial. Three daughters and five sons were born to the Nevins from 1835-1872. Only the two first-born sons survived, with five children attaining adulthood. J.W.'s maternal grandmother was a Williamson, sister of Hugh Williamson, one of the signers of the Declaration of Independence.[5]

This accounts for John's middle name of Williamson. He baptized his first grandson and gave him his name, John Nevin Sayre.[11]

The marriage of John and Martha Jenkins Nevin produced eight births. The first, a son, Wilberforce (1836-1899) died at 63 years of age. He served as Captain in the Civil War, having completed his degree at Princeton University. He was editor of the Philadelphia Press, a prominent paper of the time, and he was the assistant engineer on the Denver-Rio Grande Railroad construction. Reported to have died in the West, he is buried in Woodward Hill.

Alice, the first daughter (1837-1925), died at 88 years from a heart condition. Alice is well remembered as the organist and choir director for the College and Santee Chapel, James Street. She was a founding member and first president of The Iris Club (a name selected by the ladies in seven meetings and considerable disagreement according to the old minutes. Iris was to signify the goddess Iris, messenger for music, art, education, and cultural affairs). The Iris Club was organized in 1895 and is now one hundred years old. Alice is credited with starting the first well-baby clinic and the first kindergarten; was the first president of the newly-formed Red Cross chapter, serving 11 years; and she is the name given credit as a founding member of the Visiting Nurse Association. Alice led The Iris Club ladies in petitioning the city for paved streets. She was program chair for at least one term for Clio, a philosophic society, now 75 years old.[5, 2] Although she walked with a severe limp all her life, it did not impede her community service and social life.

Rev. Robert (1839-1906) was 75 years old when he died on a hunting trip. He, too, served in The Civil War as a captain[47], graduated from Episcopal Seminary with a letter of reference from James Buchanan at entry, went to Italy, and organized the first Protestant Church in Rome, the American Protestant Episcopal Church, sometimes called American Church or "St. Paul's within the Walls." Blanche was sometimes his hostess.

George Herbert (1840-1841), one year.[29-11]

Blanche (1841-1925), 84 years. Noted artist, poet, and sculptor and restorer of Windsor Forges. This is her biography.

Richard Cecil (1843-1867), 24 years.

Martha Finley Nevin Sayre (1845-1935), lived to 90 years old and was the only Nevin child to marry. She wed Robert Sayre, of Bethlehem, as his fourth wife. He was widowed three times and had seven children at the time of his marriage. Patty (Martha) and Robert had three sons (Cecil died in childhood), the Reverend John Nevin Sayre and Francis (Frank) Bowes Sayre. The Rev. John Sayre had two daughters, Faith and Heather, and a son, John Whitaker (1927-1981). Francis Sayre married Jessie Wilson, daughter of Woodrow Wilson, and they had three children, Frank, Eleanor, and Woodrow W. Sayre.*

John Nevin, Jr. (1846-1872), 26 years.[11, 40, 15] All of the John Williamson Nevin family are buried in the family plot at Woodward Hill Cemetery, except Rev. Robert Nevin who is buried in Arlington Cemetery, Washington, DC, and Patty who is buried with her husband in Bethlehem, PA.

---

* Tridhos Davakul, a boy from Siam, came to the States and lived with the Sayre family for seven years before returning to Siam.

⌒Three

Blanche Leaves Lancaster For Her Art Studies

Blanche went to Philadelphia to study sculpture and painting in 1862, at 21 years of age. At one time she lived at 1022 Market Street in Philadelphia. Nothing has been found that indicates that she lived with anyone. Perhaps she traveled to Italy and was stimulated to study sculpture. Her address was known at the Pennsylvania Academy of Fine Arts. However, she did not study there, but did show in their shows. In the 1876 annual exhibition at the Academy, Blanche showed her bronze statue of a Venetian beggar boy and her Cleopatra sculpture. Her main teacher was J. A. Bailey.[37] He taught only one year at the Academy. Mr. Bailey was born in Paris in 1825 and died in 1883. In Philadelphia, he followed the occupation of carving wood and marble. He produced the large statue of Washington that was placed in front of the State House in 1869 in Philadelphia. He also did portrait busts of General Grant and General Meade.[37]

Blanche had studied in Venice, Italy, by the time of the World's Columbian Exposition in 1893. The report lists Pennsylvania Women showing in the State Building, separate from the Women's Pavilion. It included Blanche Nevin.

Her marble bust of Maude Muller was in the Gallery of Honor in The Women's Pavilion. Her address was Lancaster then, and in the same year she purchased Windsor Forge. A picture of the full figured sculptures of Cinderella and Eve is included in the introduction of this book. The location of the sculptures is not known.[20] Eve was shown in

Philadelphia Centennial Exposition in 1876 and both were shown in the Chicago World Exposition in 1893.

Other well-known artists of Blanche's time are Whistler, Benjamin West, Charles Demuth, and Lloyd Mifflin of Columbia, Pennsylvania. Mifflin died during Blanche's teen years.

It was Blanche's habit to travel to warmer climates for the winter months. She is reported to have made at least five journeys just to Italy. She liked to go to Florida, but I have nothing but hearsay for the documentation.* She must have enjoyed the New Jersey shore in summer because she went to Belmar and Sea Girt more than once.[9]

Before the Chicago Exposition in 1893, there was a competition for decorative pieces to ornament the exterior of the Women's Pavilion. Blanche had entered the contest entering a model with a typewritten description. Seventeen women artists entered the competition. During the exhibition itself, Blanche Nevin had told reporters that her models were injured in transit from Philadelphia and did not do justice to her capacity for detail. These models were designed to illustrate women evolving from ancient bondage to the advanced ideas of the nineteenth century.[4] Blanche was 52 years old.

Alas, a nineteen year old, Alice Rideout was the ward of John Quinn, a well-known art collector. Miss Rideout had many friends in her home state of California. A U.S. Senator from California wrote to Mrs. Palmer, the director, the day before the contest closed. He wanted to call attention to the three groups of "plaster models" executed by Miss Rideout, saying her high character and genius had won her many friends in California, and they had taken a special interest in the matter..."[4]

The entries were kept guarded, but all to no avail because of leaks to the *Chicago Tribune*. On November 17, the *Tribune* described in detail the entries of Blanche Nevin, Kuhn Beveridge, and Enid Yandell. After two weeks, Daniel Burnham, William Pretyman, and F. M. Whitehouse, a critic and art collector selected as winner Alice Rideout. "The judges found her work to be far in advance of the remainder of those who submitted models,"[4] a comment that certainly added insult to injury for the other contestants.

But Blanche Nevin, who lost the competition for the building frieze, was represented in the Gallery of Honor with her marble bust of Maude Muller, from a poem by John Greenleaf Whittier. Much to the artist's chagrin another Maude, in plaster, was placed in the southwest corner of the Rotunda.[4]

As this information was found, and before leaving the book, *The Fair Women*, this author's curiosity about women artists in 1893 caused the scanning of the whole book. And lo! The frontispiece was a very good picture of Blanche's Cinderella and Eve statues which were in the Philadelphia Centennial Exposition and the Chicago Exposition. They seem to be lost now. A great find, since no other pictures or location information has surfaced to show some of Blanche's finer work. As for the Maude Muller bust, it seems to fit the description of the marble bust by Blanche Nevin and given to the Iris Club by William Hager some years ago. It is the one marble bust that is local and in a well-kept situation. There is no record that a bust of Eve was done, only the full nude figure adorned with flower garlands (see picture in front of book). The defining picture was made at the Philadelphia Centennial in 1876.

It is presumed that the Venetian Beggar Boy may have been an entry in a show in Venice while Blanche was living there. It was not sent to her, along with another, by her brother as recorded by one earlier writer, that is just one of the errors found in Blanche's history. That writer stated that the Venetian beggarboy and Cleopatra bust were brought out of the river, as ancient artifacts. His writing was probably hearsay.

While abroad in Massa de Carrara, Italy in 1877, Blanche sent a note to a friend, a Mrs. Kennedy, in Philadelphia thanking her for her hospitality.[36]

In June 1891, Blanche entertained her younger sister, Patty Sayre, and her two sons at Belmar on the Jersey Coast. Francis went through a period of questionable health in his early years.[9]

In 1910, Blanche was at Sea Girt, New Jersey, and at that time began the sculpture of Woodrow Wilson, president of Princeton

University. They had met earlier on a cruise to Bermuda. The completed bronze bust became the official presidential bust when Wilson became President.

Another unusual story that makes Blanche sound eccentric has to do with her attending a gathering at sister Alice's home on 227 Lancaster Avenue. On this summer day, the sculptress was dressed in blue taffeta and her ever-present armful of bracelets on each arm. Her hat was the kind of straw hat they put on horses and donkeys with holes for the ears. (I'm sure it was cooler than a lot of ladies' hats.) Sitting there on Alice's front porch, Blanche began the small clay model of a lion that became, on her front lawn at Windsor Forge, the prototype for the beautiful huge bronze lion now in Reservoir Park.[15] In Robert Simpson's later account there is an old newspaper picture with Blanche standing behind the huge clay lion.

Blanche purchased Windsor Forge, Churchtown, PA, in 1897 and lived her remaining years in her ancestral home. When Blanche came to Lancaster, after the Brunswick Hotel was built, she would take lodging there. This habit may have added to their friends' notion that the sisters didn't get along. Blanche probably had learned to like the amenities of hotel life. Another woman lived at Alice's home.** She may have been employed or roomed there. At Blanche's death, someone wrote that she was living in her apartment at the Brunswick. Blanche stayed in Lancaster to look after Alice after her heart attack, and Blanche's funeral was held in Alice's house. She died seven months before Alice, of pneumonia, in the Lancaster General Hospital. Both died in 1925 and are buried side-by-side with identical granite markers, except that Blanche's has this verse on it, selected by her nephews from one of her poems:

"Now will I pray
not for the power of beauty
race or brilliant power
But that the gift
of kindness may descend
possess and with me stay."

There was a lot of caring on Blanche's part because in 1903 another episode had Blanche going to Bethlehem to see Patty. In the words of Robert Sayre in his 1903 diary, "Blanche arrived this evening very exercised about the safety of sister Alice. Patty is in New York. Alice had sailed for Jamaica nine days earlier on the boat *Constitution*. (His handwriting was growing poor; he died two years later believing he had undiagnosed cancer.) Blanche had learned of the severe hurricane that struck the island on the 11th. She had cabled Secretary Hay to see if any word could be gotten from the U.S. Consul. So on August 17 there was still no response. My cablegram brought no response. Patty and Blanche by then very distressed. We decided Blanche should go to the docks as planned August 18 to see if Alice returned. I think she will. Patty had received a telegram from Alice just before the hurricane. On the 19th Patty received a telegram from Blanche that Alice and Elsie Beacher arrived in good shape."[9]

Patty had shared a letter with Blanche that Reverend Robert had arrived from Italy. And this elderly diarist concluded, "Much cause for thankfulness."[40] On the 21st he wrote that Patty went to Lancaster to visit Alice and Robert. Blanche joined them.

Patty and Blanche held memberships in some New York clubs and in Philadelphia. Alice had visited women's clubs in several cities presumably before forming the Iris Club in Lancaster. In 1905, Patty and Blanche went to New York to Christmas shop, one of many New York trips.

At one point in Sayre's diary, Friday, January 23, 1903, he noted that Blanche came to visit the Sayres, and on Saturday had stayed in bed all day. In *The Glad Adventure*, the autobiography of Francis Bowes Sayre, the youngest nephew, he wrote of his Aunt Blanche singing to him when he was a child, accompanying herself on her guitar.

This family involvement created a significant romantic event in three lives. Young Francis Bowes Sayre was coming to Windsor Forge on his Easter break from Princeton about 1910. Blanche invited Jessie Wilson, whom she met on the 1907 cruise to Bermuda as Jessie traveled with her parents. The Wilsons were repeating a trip Woodrow had made the year before by himself when there was a rift in his first marriage. The Wilsons had lost a child and the mourning may have contributed to the problem.[31]

Jessie arrived and was welcomed by Aunt Blanche, singing her poem she wrote for her visit, at the beautiful front door of Windsor Forge. The whole poem "Jessie, Come In" is included in the poetry chapter later in this book.

The young people took buggy rides around the countryside, went on picnics in the pastoral surrounding area, drove to Lancaster to see Wild Bill Cody Wild West Show, and walked along the headwaters of the Conestoga River.

They were married in the East Room of the White House, November 25, 1913, after Woodrow Wilson became President. Their first two children, a boy and a girl, were born in the White House.[31] Their third child was born while they were in Siam, now Thailand, as Francis served a great need in helping Siam open trade with the world. He also served as U.S. High Commissioner of the Phillippine Territory, as diplomat. He was Commissioner of Corrections for the State of New York when he was appointed Assistant Secretary of State under Stettinius and Cordell Hull during Franklin D. Roosevelt's third term. Jessie died after 15 years of marriage, and Francis married a widow, a Mrs. Graves, in 1937, while Assistant Secretary of State.[31, 8]

Blanche traveled most of Europe and apparently attained membership in the Royal Art Societies in Britain and Italy — no small feat for a woman artist. She lived and studied in China and Japan, giving the impression she did not just pass through. Going to Italy was natural for her since her brother, Reverend Robert Nevin, resided in Rome. He had bought a church and organized St. Paul's American Protestant Episcopal Church in Rome. It was located in the new quarter of the city, at that time, on the Via Nazionale. Architect G. E. Street was the designer. In a letter to James Buchanan, his friend, he said he paid $19,000, but needed to raise $43,000 for restoration. It had a size of

132 feet by 64 feet of floor space, which allowed for 750 seats. The height to the cross on the facade was 70 feet. In another letter, he explained that his congregation was very transient because many American tourists came to the church, and he did not have a stable income from parishioners. When Robert came back to the United States, he had an address in the Episcopal Rooms, Philadelphia, in 1872. He came on a fundraising tour. Robert died on a hunting trip and is buried in Arlington Cemetery.[36]

Blanche had other places where she lived and studied in Italy. It seems she would rent a studio in different areas to secure marble and be near another of her instructors. She was beginning the General Muhlenberg statue in Carrara, where she had gone to purchase fine marble, and wrote a friend, Mrs. Kennedy, of how the cold and marble dust were making her hands sore. She completed Muhlenberg at Windsor Forge.[52]

In 1877, Blanche was working in Carrara, two years before the Muhlenberg Commission from the State of Pennsylvania's first Art Commission. It was appointed by Governor Hartranft in response to Statuary Hall and the U.S. Government's invitation to states to provide important sculptures for the Hall (the committee report provided by Statuary Hall will be included in its entirety since other local, prominent names appear in the committee). In a letter that Blanche sent to her friend, Mrs. Sherman, she asked if Mr. Rogers had come abroad. She said Wilberforce, her eldest brother and editor of the Philadelphia Press, was in Paris and that he and Rev. Robert in Rome were writing every few days to her.[52] This, again, indicates that she was very involved with her family, contrary to some beliefs held by people in her hometown of Lancaster.

Another of Blanche's notes, written on May 1, 1910, was addressed to a Mr. Jordan, and in her words, "Windsor Forge, Churchtown, Lancaster County, Pennsylvania. I shall be very pleased to see you and Governor Pennypacker on Saturday, May 3, to outdoor lunch (al fresco) at one. If either of you have a car it might be very easy to get here via Downingtown and Honeybrook, etc. There is a telegraph, but I have the Bell Telephone. In the country I am the real thing, not simply suburban, and we have natural conveniences. Sincerely yours, May 1, 1910. Blanche Nevin."

This may not have been to commission a sculpture, but to see Blanche's household items. It was reported she had offered everything to the Pennsylvania Historical Society. Mr. Jordan is credited with founding the P.H.S. and Governor Pennypacker was president of the P.H.S. for some time. His autobiography tells of his activity with P.H.S.[53]

From Blanche's directions in her reply it would appear that the Governor was living at Pennypacker Mills, near Schwenksville, Pennsylvania. It was his summer place while in office; then he made it his permanent residence, which is now a house museum open to the public.

In another trip, a search of the Jordan and Pennypacker files revealed nothing to indicate the exact reason for their visit to Windsor Forge.

---

* Faith Schindler had poetry written by Blanche while she was in Florida—a last minute find.

**In Alice's will, a cousin with two children and the last name Wiley were to stay in the house with all servants until all bequests were completed. The cousin inherited several thousand dollars.

Four

Sculptures By Blanche Nevin

The Most Noted Sculpture

lanche was commissioned by the State of Pennsylvania, not the D.A.R., Daughters of the Revolution, as at least one writer had written. Statuary Hall provided the typed copy of the first Pennsylvania Art Commission's report to Governor Hartranft. The Commission did not rush into any decision, as their meetings, called by Simon Cameron, ranged from 1877 to the final report in 1879.

Statuary Hall had just been built, and all the states were invited to contribute statues of important "historic" figures. The committee report is included in the special interest section because of the noted people on the Commission.

Lorado Taft, author of "History of American Sculpture" seemed unaware of the realistic portrayals that Blanche sculpted. He called General Muhlenberg "an insignificant and effeminate figure in a colonial wig and garb."[32]

Taft didn't extend his search to find what General Muhlenberg's actual size was—uniform and all. In Muhlenberg's biography, he is described as medium height and at that time that was little more than what short is now. In his picture and description, he appears to have been a somewhat slight man, physically speaking.

This all added to his dramatic, demonstrative act in his pulpit in Woodstock, Virginia, when at the end of a rather patriotic sermon he flung open his robe and exposed his Revolutionary War uniform. He told the congregation that he had joined the Revolutionary forces and encouraged others to enlist. Three hundred did on the spot or later that day. What he may have lacked in stature he made up for with his passionate patriotism.[51]

Persons who visit Statuary Hall will find many distorted sizes in the other sculptures, to somehow instill importance, even having extra high pedestals.General Muhlenberg is in good company in the entrance alcove. The other three figures are realistic sizes as well.

In the various writings that the people wrote of Blanche, there were different prices set that Blanche was paid. One person said $15,000, several said $5,000, and the art commission recommended $7,500 and had contracts signed with the artists, Blanche Nevin for General Peter Muhlenberg, whose full name is Reverend John Peter Gabriel Muhlenberg (he evidently used Peter to distinguish him from his illustrious father) and Howard Roberts to sculpt Robert Fulton for $7,500. Now, whether the legislature appropriated the recommended amount is another search. There was a period of eight years from the date of the contract with the Art Commission until the installation of the statue in Statuary Hall. (The Art Commission report is in the appendix.)

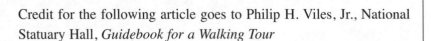

Credit for the following article goes to Philip H. Viles, Jr., National Statuary Hall, *Guidebook for a Walking Tour*

JOHN P. G. MUHLENBERG

Lutheran Pastor, Revolutionary War General, Representative and
  Senator
Born: Trappe, PA, on October 1, 1746
Died: Gray's Ferry, Montgomery County, PA, on October 1, 1807
Interred: Trappe, PA

John Peter Gabriel Muhlenberg, a Pennsylvania native, was a Virginia clergyman and state legislator before fighting in the Revolutionary War. He was a vital aide to Washington and a hero when he returned to Pennsylvania. His later years were spent in public service.

Muhlenberg attended the Academy of Philadelphia (later the University of Pennsylvania) and then studied in the University of Halle, Germany, 1763-66. He studied theology and was ordained in 1768, becoming pastor of Lutheran churches in New Germantown and Bedminster, New Jersey, serving as his father's assistant.

In 1771, he accepted a call to the German Lutheran Congregation at Woodstock, Virginia. To gain the advantages of clergyman of the Anglican Church, he went to England and was ordained a priest on April 23, 1772, by the Bishop of London. Muhlenberg began work at Woodstock in the late summer or early autumn of 1772, and was soon the leader of the community.

In 1774, he was elected to the Virginia House of Burgesses and in January 1776, raised and commanded the Eighth Virginia Regiment. In February 1777, he was commissioned Brigadier-General in the Continental Army. He was in numerous Revolutionary War battles. In late 1779, General Washington sent him to Virginia to take military command of that state and Muhlenberg figured in every major campaign afterwards. In October 1781, he and his men were a vital part of the pressure which persuaded Cornwallis to surrender at Yorktown. At the close of the war (September 30, 1783) Muhlenberg was brevetted

Major-General.

After the war, he settled his affairs in Virginia and went to Philadelphia in late 1783, where he was said to be a hero. He held high offices in Pennsylvania, including the Vice Presidency (Benjamin Franklin was President) from 1785 to 1788. He was elected to represent his Pennsylvania district in the First, Third, and Sixth Congresses. In 1790, he had been a member of the State Constitutional Convention for Pennsylvania.

On February 18, 1801, he was elected to the United States Senate but resigned four months later to be appointed Supervisor of Revenue for Philadelphia. In 1802, he became Collector of Customs for Philadelphia, a post he held until his death. His son, his brother, his nephew, his great-great-grand-nephew all served in Congress, representing Pennsylvania.

NAMES OF BLANCHE'S SCULPTURES

It is considered an incomplete list. The first seven are located and being preserved:

1. General John Peter Gabriel Muhlenberg, a realistic statue in marble of a small-statured man. Statuary Hall 1907.

2. Woodrow Wilson, a bust, sculpted from life. The original bronze is in the US Capitol. Copies have been placed in the other educational institutions that Woodrow Wilson had been connected to in some office. Blanche began the clay model at Sea Girt, NJ, when she and the Wilsons were at their summer places. For the record, Blanche has two sculptures in the nation's Capitol.

3. A bust of a young girl, thought for a while to be Eve. Since finding the picture showing Eve as full standing nude draped with garlands, we now think the bust is Maude Muller in marble. It is the bust given to the Iris Club by Nathaniel Hager's father, William Hager. John Hager, from Lancaster, served on the first Art Commission with Simon Cameron and others so he would have known Blanche's work. The bust was shown in The Philadelphia Centennial Exposition 1876 and the Chicago World Exposition in 1893. It is in the library of the Iris Club.

4. The beautiful bronze lion in Reservoir Park. Blanche sculpted the lion and signed it in memory of her father, Reverend John W. Nevin, in 1905. The fountain basin has an iron fence around it and there are brass name plates of historic persons. The names still there in 1994 are Lindley Murray, Benjamin West, James Bachman, and Robert Fulton. One name couldn't be read, and one plate is missing.

5. The horse fountain is a delicate marble cross with flower adornment and is the first piece that Blanche signed. It was in honor of

her mother, Martha Jenkins Nevin. It was designed with a basin that caught the fountain flow so that horses could drink from it. Many cities had horse fountains, sometimes with a lower basin for small animals. This was a late 1700-1800 kind of animal rights movement around the country. The horse fountain is located in the "V" space where West Orange comes to meet Columbia Avenue before it becomes West King Street. Coming in from Columbia you have a good view of the horse fountain. The horse fountain was given to Lancaster in 1898, seven years before the lion fountain in Reservoir Park.

6. Three of Blanche's creations are on the front lawn of Windsor Forge. The two English lions, with a paw holding a shield, flank the beautiful front entrance. They are of some granular concrete-like material over metal armature. On pedestals, they have guarded the doorway for at least 96 years. The armature is beginning to show through from weathering.

7. The Buddha sits to the right on the front lawn and is to represent Ghatama. It has the same material in the work as the lions it appears. It is interesting that the Buddha's hair seems to be done in a Greco-Roman flatcurl style. This was Blanche's souvenir of her China and Japan sojourn as she traveled the world. The story of the making of the Buddha parallels that of making the model for the large bronze lion for the park. At one time then the lion model of clay was at the other side of the front entrance and the Buddha was across the front on the other side. Did people drive to see the sculptures?

8. Theodore Roosevelt's bust has not been located at this writing, but there is a picture of the bust on the marble pedestal in front of the living room fireplace in Windsor Forges.

9. President McKinley is probably the other bust opposite Theodore Roosevelt, as they flank the beautiful fireplace mantel. The two

brown marble pedestals appear to be the two in the Iris Club for some years. The McKinley bust is not located.

10. Catherine Carmichael Jenkins, grandmother of Blanche, was recorded as a bust and reportedly owned by Blanche's sister, Alice Nevin (1926). In Alice's estate inventory a bust on a pedestal is listed, but location now is unknown.

11. The Venetian Beggar boy was a bronze shown by Blanche in the Pennsylvania Academy of Fine Arts show in 1876.[62] Location unknown.

12. Cleopatra—a bust was also shown in the Academy show of 1876.[62] Location unknown.

13. Eve—the standing nude figure was shown in the Pennsylvania Academy of Fine Art show in 1876 and the Chicago Exposition. Location unknown. May have been a plaster model.[62]

14. Cinderella was a sitting, full-size figure in a dress reading a letter (invitation). This sculpture, with Eve, is pictured as they were displayed at the Chicago Exposition in 1893. Location unknown.

15. The Sphinx.[52] Not located.

16. Victory—a restoration of the Naples torso.[52] Not located.

17. Lincoln bust.[52] Not located.

18. Winged Peace—this was the sculpture Blanche was working on at her death. She had wished to complete it for a gift to the US Government.[52] Location is unknown.

It is hoped that the printing of this biography of Blanche will bring some more into the present knowledge of the artist's career work.

The only sculptures known at the beginning of the research were the lion in the park, horse fountain, and the three pieces on Windsor Forge lawn.

Rev. Amos Seldomridge remembers a big chest on the third floor of Windsor Mansion that held many pretty, little angels. The closet was lighted only by flashlight and was off the bedroom Blanche used with the "King's Bed" she imported.

The Lion In The Park

Photographs

The late Miss Blanche Nevin
Photo Courtesy of **Lancaster Sunday News**

Blanche photographed beside her self-portait in 1921.
She was 81 years old.
(Photo reproduction by Rick Hertzler)

Once thought to be the statue of Eve, this sculpture is believed to be the Maud Muller.
It is currently in the library of the Iris Club House.

Two views of General Muhlenberg

Windsor Forge Mansion, 1996
English Lions and Buddha date around 1903-1909

Horse fountain sculpted and given to the City of Lancaster in honor of Blanche's mother in 1888.

Above the fountain it reads, "Ho! Ye who thirst."

Another view of the Lion.

Windsor Mansion
Front of Windsor Forge Mansion with Pergola to right.

Windsor Mansion— rear view
Terraced rear gardens

Miss Blanche Nevin
Robert Simpson wrote that this is a trick picture with the full face view of Blanche and four other views. The eyes crinkle in a smile of enjoyment.

King's bed in "haunted" bedroom

Lex Pax fireplace and stove used as Blanche's heater.
Lost sculptures, McKinley and Theodore Roosevelt.

Imported desk of several carved woods

The offical bronze bust of the Woodrow Wilson presidency.

At her death in 1925 Blanche was working on her sculpture of "Peace." She wished to give it to the nation when completed.

*Blanche painting the "Doomed Tree," subject of one
of her poem booklets.*

"The Doomed Tree"
Photo from the painting by Miss Blanche Nevin
Recent find by Jerald Martin

The Venetian mirror that Blanche purchased as she traveled.

**Blanche sculpted Teddy Roosevelt and also
had this piece of furniture that came into vogue during the
presidency of Theodore Roosevelt 1901—1909.**

Blanche, shown here in her most remembered photograph, was noted for her flair for dressing, using color and jewelry freely.

Six

Blanche's Poetry Anthology

Blanche's poetry that has been found. The first poem was illustrated with tiny silhouettes that define the meaning of each verse.

Great Grandma's Looking Glass

by Blanche Nevin
and Illustrated by
Annis Dunbar Jenkins

New York
Robert Grier Cooke, Inc.

DEDICATED TO
THE GHOSTS OF WINDSOR FORGES
POLITELY
BY THEIR PRESENT PROPRIETOR
BLANCHE NEVIN

Great Grandma's Looking Glass

Old mirror hanging on my wall,
Dreaming to-night, dost thou recall
The dramas thou hast seen to pass
And swallowed deep, my looking-glass?

In thy weird depths in vain I gaze,
Seeking reflex of thy young days,

The aspect of my great-grand-dame,
The generations since that came
Thou hast reflected in each mood—
Joy, hope, grief, humor bad or good.

Here came the gay, their powdered hair,
Bedecked for ball, piled high in air.
Here came the men in queues and laces
And satin vests, to shave their faces.

And here they held the babies high
To quiet them when they did cry.
To thee the bachelor came to prink
When of his wooing he did think.

To thee, shy glancing thro' their curls,
On Hallowe'en came peeping girls.

And many a bride forth—going, bright,
Here saw herself in shinning white,
Who, after—years, all worn and pale,
Came back to drape her widow's veil.

Before thee, swollen with tears and pain,
Dimmed eyes have striven to dry again
As mourners dressed to meet the call
To follow the grim funeral pall.
Perchance, held o'er the bed of death,
Thy face was dulled by dying breath.

Sagacious mirror, that dost know
Such histories of joy and woe—
That watched the fact of human lives,
Of parents, children, husbands, wives—
Thou awest and thou bafflest me.
Why is it that I cannot see,
Strain as I will, the ghostly faces
Thou holdest deep in thine embraces?
The faces in their life and laughter,
The ancestors I follow after?

Alack! The shadowy troop have gone.
The only face left is my own.
Mine are the only eyes I see
Pensively gazing out at me.
I cannot call the vanished back.
And I? I follow in their track.
Why once they were, why now am I,
To understand I will not try.

In 1903 after the sudden death of her horse, "Champagne" from colic, Blanche wrote a memorial poem about him called "The Last Whinny."

> Good-bye Champagne, my pretty Champagne,
> With the white tail and flowing mane,
> Good-by, forever and ever again.
> Friends were we through the summer weather,
> Climbing the mountain roads together,
> Nipping buds in the heart of the wood,
> I sang, you whinnied, each understood,
> And the sky was blue and life was good.
>
> There were the streams and under the dint
> of your slender hoofs the fragrant mint;
> There was the moss, and the wild grape vine,
> The rhododendron, laurel and pine,
> The honeysuckle, the columbine.
>
> Remote from struggle, away from care,
> Peace profound in the rarefied air;
> Without temptation to sin—no need
> To worry ourselves with anxious creed;
> The very God seemed with us indeed.
>
> Good-by, Champagne, my pretty Champagne,
> With the white tail, and the foaming mane,
> Sad on the mountain sobs the rain.
>
> It's likely I'll go to Heaven some day,
> When this poor body is sloughed away,
> If I am good and absolved of sin,
> But that is a goal you cannot win;
> For Heaven they don't let horses in.

I am glad you do not understand
That this is the last touch of my hand;
That into Heaven you cannot get,
That you don't know why my cheeks are wet
As you bend to me your neck to pet.
Now here are queries to pose the knowledge
Of each trustee of Carnegie's college:
Why I have a soul and you have none;
Why you must perish, and I go on.
Which to day is the pitiful one?

Happy it is in Heaven, no doubt,
Yet, surely, some day, I will look out;
Mine eyes through infinite space will strain
For a glint of snowy tail and mane,
As you whinny, whinny, once again,

Good-by, Champagne, my pretty Champagne,
With the white tail, and the foaming mane,
Out of the shadows whinny again!

"One Usual Day" by Blanche Nevin was copied in total by Mr. Robert Simpson, of Churchtown, in his *Rambler* column. Many of her poems are quoted in part in the old annals, so finding the whole poem has been very fulfilling for the purpose of this book.

ONE USUAL DAY
Blanche Nevin 1916

Our rooster crowing and the flies
Woke me at dawn, I russed my eyes,
And yawned and curled my toes, and then
I tried to go to sleep again

Vainly, for I could doze no more,
I stared at "Yankee" on the floor,
And at the walls where cracks in places
Resembled silhouettes of faces.
Then Hannah brought my breakfast up
Puffed rice, raw eggs, and coffee-cup.

Some mornings at my window pane
A bird taps — there he is again
"Get ready, B," he seems to say
"To fly to heaven with me today."
But as you know
        I do not go.
But get up, dress, and say my prayers
And wind my watch, and go down stairs.

There on the porch I idly sit
And gaze upon my view a bit;
Where the Welsh Mountains guard and rally
Our fertile Conestoga Valley;
The woods, the streams, the meadowed plain

The corn, the golden field of grain
All swathed in misty morning air
As if the whole earth hushed
As shrouded Arabs greet the sun
When early morning has begun.

But waxing day reminds us we
Must get to work and busy be.
To keep comforts in this life
Demands incessant strain and strife.
How letters do accumulate
My desk and pen, and ink await
Attention, concentration, and
My busy chirographic hand.
One of the tasks of Windsor summers
Is writing billet doux to plumbers.
They answering send due bills, and so
We keep things lively at P.O.

Some people from the city call
The country dull — Why not at all.
We have excitements every day
Springing upon us in a way.
Early a voice thrills through the house
"The trap has caught another mouse."
Contentment fills my vengeful breast,
Those plaguey mice are such a pest.
They eat my cake and even soap.
With baking powder mixed, I hope
Some day to get a fine result
And give those mice a cat-a-pult.

Then "Bob" breaks halter and instanter
Lopes off in glorious, free-legged canter.

Over the lawns, and garden bends
Over the terrace he treads.
(Our only groom has gone away
To help his father make the hay.)
To catch him now what shall we do?
Hannah and I his flight pursue
With sticks, Ho, Ho's and plates of meal;
And "Yankee" clattering at his heel.
A neighbor boy who sees the fuss
Deserts his plow to succor us.
And with experienced skill is able
To catch and lead him to the stable.

One of those cases rare, when man
Does better than a woman can.

Excitement? In what city street
So fine a horse race would you meet?

The gentleman who left his work
To aid the dames, is called Sam Shirk,
Shirk is his name, but not his nature
He far excels his nomen-clature
And is a most industrious "Crayture."

Bob harnessed in the run-about
To do my errands takes me out.
Shakes his abbreviated tail
And trots to Churchtown for the mail.
There at the Post I have a chat
With neighbor this, or neighbor that,
And if by chance I cast a glance
Across the street, or turn my head
I see "God's Acre" of the dead,

The village graveyard where gray stones
Cover my own forefather's bones.

A very little time ago
They know the streets which now we know.
and now we live, and now we walk
And now we drive, and now we talk,
And powerless they for good or ill,
They lie so deep, they lie so still!
If they had not begotten me
Perplexing thought, where would I be?
Perhaps in the empyrean blue
With angels looking down at you,
Or maybe an electron rife
With self-evolved ebullient life.
But "ours is not to reason why"
Thought only tangles if we try,
So home we drive, and there proceed
Our letters and news to read.

And every day they print so much
With the wide world we keep in touch,
Serene in easy chair, I read
How foes conflict and nations bleed,
Like wildcats fighting, at the cost
Of centuries of labor lost;
How politicians in the race
For power, for wealth, for ruling place
Squabble and scratch, deceive and lie;
Our men all fight, I wonder why?
Perhaps because they have not yet
Done justice to the suffragette.
Studied by men and women, too,
From widely different points of view

All questions which in equal share
Child, man and woman all must bear,
Must be well sifted and more fit
If man was helped by woman's wit.
We might have peace at last, because
We could have less lop-sided laws.

The opera of the world to sing
All by male voices, is a thing
Ambitious, but God gave us grace
To stand all tenor and all bass.
A sweet contralto and soprano
Might make race music more piano;
Ah! It would be a perfect thing
If all in harmony would sing
In the full chorus of the glee
Which represents humanity!
For bass and tenor, while admired
Leave something still to be desired.
"Revenons a nos moutons" —See
How apt that phraseology
Doth with bucolic fete agree.
"Revenons a nos moutons," then
And take newspaper up again,
Someone has fled to foreign lands
With money trusted in his hands;
Another shot his wife's heart through
And killed his babies quite a few,
Another to enlarge his life
Ran off with someone else's wife

And pictured here upon the page
A half nude actress all the rage
A nation ruler, old and gray

Besides a modern divorcee,
A bigamist; a modest bride
Hobnobbing, smirking side by side,
All this the usual hashed up diet
I note, emotionally quiet.
For I have read the same things oe'r
The day before, and day before.

But Jubilate! All is not —
Such a malodorous, nasty rot,
For here and there a brighter line
Illumes the items, something fine.
Frequent, in deeds we read about,
Nobility of soul shines out.
Some spark divine of sacrifice

Strength amid cowardice and vice
Some hand stretches from the careless crowd
To help the fallen, raise the bowed,
Always some fight to shun the evil,
To help the Lord, and chase the devil.

Who does not travel with the crowd
Is jeered at hard, is jeered at loud.
The wit he had, the grit he had
Is unperceived, man call him mad.
A few look on and thank the Lord
For giving us our Henry Ford.

And so wherever good is seen
Amidst the sordid and the mean
Thought joyful through our head flashes
God is not dead, God is not dead!

High noon, the farmer's dinner bell
Rings, and the dogs set up a yell.
High noon, we go and take our bite
Of goodly fare with appetite.
Of that substantial country fare
There is enough and some to spare
For tramps perhaps just out of jail.
Life's derelicts, the ones who fail.
Perhaps they do not earn their bread;
Neither do we if truth were said.
Perhaps they lack the wit to try —
Ability! — and so do I.
Perhaps their failures represent
Heredity — environment.

There sit ye down beneath a tree
A little while and rest with me.
And "Yankee" do not groul or bite,
I bid you try to be polite.
Dirt you don't like, or rags, it's true.
But you are not a parvenu.
"A dog that's down you must not kick;"
That is a snobbish, vulgar trick.

The hours of every day unclose
As do the petals of a rose;
In its deep heart unfolding our

Rich possibilities and power.
There hides all ready to advance
Our opportunity and chance.
Grief, joy, pain, happiness perdu
Are awaiting there for me or you.
Take humbly what we can and call

On the dear Lord to bless it all.

We'll have to skip the afternoon;
Pleasant it was, but over soon.
Enough! You might get tired of me
And ho, how dreadful that would be!
But at its close I heave a sigh
Compunctions that so little I
Have done to help the general good.
Full penitential is my mood,
But I take heart — dismiss my sorrow,
Hoping I will reform tomorrow.

And duty now my memory quickens;
I must go out and feed my chickens.

One rooster in our flock is quite
Remarkable — he's so polite.
He is a most distinguished fellow,
With crimson comb and beak deep yellow.
On handsome lines his form is built.
He holds his head with royal tilt.
Come, Sir Charles Grandison, and take
Out of my hand this piece of cake.
Sir Charles is hatched from noble greed,
And is a gentleman indeed.
Unselfish, chivalrous, he strives
Before himself to feed his wives;
Calls them to him, puts at their feet
The rarest scraps he has to eat.
His instincts fine suggest that maybe
He knows the code of Hammurabi.
Oh, metamorphosed could he be
From some remote far ancestry?

Once potentate who lavished bounty;
Now, crowing in Lancaster County?
Perhaps a weird reincarnation
From some remotely foreign nation,
Who learned politeness in his feeding
From Egypt or from India's breeding.

Tell me, Sir Charles, is this true
Suspicion which I have of you?
Your pretty manners can you trace
Back to some pre-historic race?
He turned his head without reply,
Unblinking was his onyx eye,
Like some of us, I rather guess,
He felt more than he could express;
He stretched his neck and open beak
And seemed as if about to speak
Then gave a prepotential crow,
Exactly like Old Pharaoh!

The night comes on, the day is done;
Sinks in the sky the golden sun.
Oblique cross the emerald green
His javelins of light are seen.
Into life's rag-bag tossed away
Are all our actions of today;
Patches and scraps to be pulled out
When our career is talked about,
Which, pieced together, quilted whole,
Will show the pattern of our soul.

The night is here, we go to rest,
And all the garrulous birds seek nest;
Then to the tunes of night resilient

The dancing fireflies sparkle brilliant.
Good night, good night, the day is done,
And so — Good-bye to every one.

This tree stood on the bank of the Conestoga in Miss Nevin's meadow. It was a favorite resort of the roving westons of the road. Many a man built a fire on the south leeward side of this oak tree to make his coffee. Gradually the fire ate into the trunk until it was a mere shell, and at last, the dry shell too caught fire, and the old oak toppled over. The poem was written in 1912.

THE DOOMED TREE

Kind people, good people, listen to me
Crooning the dirge of a dying old tree.

All the rest gone,
Standing alone
The oak of past centuries burns to the bone.

'Twas in the night,
Some witless wight,
Some poacher skulking from the honest light
Beside the water of the nether brook
To catch his rabbit or his food to cook
Lit in these ancient roots a hidden fire,
Which caught the pith above, and mounting higher
Smouldered within the trunk.
When morning broke
We, sorry, saw thence issuing clouds of smoke.
Nor all the water poured from Angelo's pails*
To check or quench that fatal fire avails.

That oak! The last of the vast forest here
When first arrived our earliest pioneer.
When friendly Indians made
Camp underneath its shade,
When hammock-swung papoose crowed and played

Or rolled in tent, or into dugout strayed.
Around this trunk the grazing buck has prowled,
And catamount and strange wild beasts have growled,
And flocks of wild geese hushed their strident squak,
Struck by stone arrow or hurled tomahawk.
Ere blunderbuss and musket ball and shot
Drove those archaic weapons from the spot.

Here in Springtime frog and katy-did
Make mellow music, and the nests are hid
Of migratory birds. Here whip-poor-wills
And orioles, and amatory trills
And all the starry sky vibrating thrills.

We took the land, the streams, the forest trees,
And this lone oak is all that's left of these.
Stronger of fibre this alone long-lived
The changes all about it has survived.
    Has known of new-born breath,
    Of vanishments of death,
As generations came and went beneath.

Patience, courage, and the ringing axe,
And sinewy arms, and burden-bearing backs
    Cleared fertile field
    For the rich yield
Of crops of corn, of hay, of oats, of wheat.
Then came the iron forges and the beat
And throb of bellows. And the enterprise
Of venturous business. And stone houses rise,
And fortunes, gradual swell and flourish then,
Wrought by the blows of the Welsh hammermen
    Bustle and shout
    Were all about,

And noise, and song, and hearty cheer rang out,
While stalwart teamsters prod their jaded teams
To ford the dam breast and the swollen streams.
Then, doubtless, was that black horse reared and sold
Which King George bought for twelve good pounds of
gold.

Later those teams, with horseshoes laden down,
To General Morgan went, to Reading town.

Here the fife shrilled
    When Continentals drilled,
As all the land awoke
    To shift the British yoke.

Souls of the brave, whose bodies lie in dust,
Forgotten, perishing, as a valor must,
To check the arrogance of human lust,
God has some special place for ye, we trust.

And little wading feet,
    Out of this calm retreat,
Went forward, eagerly the world to meet,
And waded into waters deeper far
    And bitterer than the Conestoga's are.

Into this wilderness, as it was then
Came riding from the city gentlemen
Came Hannah Flower, came the young William Penn
Who tore his buckskin breeches by the way
But had them mended 'ere he rode away.

Hither came brides. Rebecca Meredith,
Forsaking all her Philadelphia kith

And kin, grandchild of Colonel Rush, who fled
After the Roundheads cut off King Charles' head
Of Cromwell's army he, of stubborn faith,
Whose daughter—so the ancient bible saith—
Was the first white girl born of Englishman
Within the settlement of William Penn.

And our Rebecca was a winsome maid;
Her wedding dress was of sky blue brocade
'Broidered with gold. Her riding horse was white,
With saddle crimson velvet all bedight,
It used to kneel down at her little feet
And from her lily hand take sugar sweet.

Then Martha Armour.** She who put to flight
And foiled by strategy the Doanes one night.
She was industrious, very good and wise.
Tradition has it that she made the pies,
Which argues for ability, at least;
For good pies are the crowning of the feast.

She was the one
     Who saved her little son
From drowning in a well.
     How it was done
     No one can tell

Coming in one day from harvesting the hay
Men found her by the old well, where she lay
In a dead faint, her baby in her arms
Held tight, and screaming, full of vague alarms.
They "brought her to,"
But all she knew was that she saw the child

Fall in the well. Then she went wild.
This only she remembered, nothing more;
But both were wringing wet, and bruised and sore.
How she got down, and up, none knew. 'Twas thought
Climbing, the baby in her teeth was brought—
 Her mother-wit
 Had managed it.

Then Catherine Carmichael, orphaned young,
But sired by him of Presbyterian tongue,
And Argyle blood who risked his life to save,
At Valley Forge, our army from the grave.
Whose head the British put a price upon
For carrying aid to General Washington.
His heart with love of liberty was full,
His sermons, to speak truth, were rather dull.

All passes, we progressing and perforce
Must follow on, unwitting of our course.
The forges went, when steam's advancing hour
Destroyed the value of the water power.
Scotch, Welsch, and English to the Germans yield
Their cleared plantations, meadow land and field.
For soon or late Life's fateful shifting sands
Put our possessions into other hands.

One to another we have given place—
People of different types, of varied race,
Up in the churchyard—if one cares to go—
You see the tombs and headstones in a row.
We vanished one by one—
Father and son and son—
Unmoved, more strong than they, the tree lived on.

I would I were a tree, that cannot feel
Or suffer from the blow of tongue or steel.
Unthrilled by joy, unmoved by human pain,
Tossing its branch in sunshine and in rain,
Shedding its leaves to put them forth again.

What would life be if we could only know
How little matters either joy or woe?
    So soon we pass
    Under the grass
And end this spasm we call life alas!

Even a tree must fall at last. And, hark,
I hear the wrenching of the trunk and bark!
With rustle crepitant, with crackling sound
The shattered tree falls thundering to the ground.

Better that stroke of axe, than smoke
Had laid thee low, my gallant oak.

Whatever meanings to its life belong
Are ended with this tributary song.

All gentle people who have held with me
This requiem over an old forest tree,
Thanks for your courtesy. God give you grace!
And send you merry Christmas in each time and place.

---

* Angelo was the young Italian man Blanche brought from Italy. His
English had improved and he went to Chicago after he spent a winter
with Robert Simpson, when Blanche went to warmer climate. The
last Mr. Simpson heard, Angelo Pellichelli was teaching at a university in Chicago.

**Blanche's great, great grandfather, David Jenkins, married Martha Armour, daughter of General Robert Armour of Pequea, around 1777.

Recently, while this writing was in progress, Jerald Martin was given some of Blanche's poetry booklets by a friend of Robert Simpson's, for the Churchtown Historical Society archives. Jerald shared the complete poem for this chapter, and so you may read it in its entirety.

Blanche was born in Mercersburg on Linden Avenue. She may have written this before she left Mercersburg at 12 years old. It was located in the "Old Mercersburg," by the Women's Club of Mercersburg. The Nevins lived there from 1840-1853.

MY HEART IS WEARY FOR THE LILIES

My heart is weary for the lilies. Oh,
That I might wander far beyond the snow
And find the garden where the lilies grow!

Lilies, clean silver lilies to illume
And glorify the dimness of my room,
Lilies of light to penetrate the gloom.

Not the bright roses of the shining day;
Roses are fittest when the hour is gay;
For holy-hearted lilies now I pray.

Once in the summer time I wooed the Rose,
Drank its perfume and sorrowed when it froze;
Now I want only lilies—and repose.

Christ! Make thine Easter lilies bloom again!
See, how thy poor are crying out in pain,
And all the land is full of snow and rain.

Sharp is the wind, and cutting is the sleet,
Cold and unclean we walk the dreary street;
Cold and unclean the mire about our feet.

In vain we turn for hope toward thy sky;
Clouds are so dense, and heaven—alas—so high

No sun shines visible to human eye.
Death lurks for victims in the poisonous air,
Disease is prowling near us everywhere,
And Pestilence growls threatening from his lair.

Show us, O Thou who once removed our stain,
We need not pray for purity in vain!
Christ, bid thy solemn lilies bloom again.

— Blanche Nevin.

This poem is included in the "Souvenir of the Pilgrimage of the Historical Society of Berks County to Windsor Forges," which is included in this book as part of Blanche's writings (September 2, 1921) in the Appendix.

TO MY DOOR
By: Miss Blanche Nevin

If genius, or the studious brain
By happy chance, should kindly deign
To tap upon thy wooden side,
Open, my door, fly open wide.

To gentle courtesy, to grace,
To wit, good heart, and smiling face;
To the frank brow, the honest hand,
Open, my door, wide open stand.

To love, to friendship and to truth,
To interesting age, or youth;
To worthy rich or worthy poor,
Stand ever open wide, my door.

If formal folk would visit make
Receive them for politeness sake;
But to the stupid or the bore
Creak slowly on thy hinge, my door.

If fate unkind should ever send
Hypocrisy in guise of friend,
If insincerity should knock
Tighten thy lock, tighten thy lock.

Strengthen thy bolts against the bad,
Keep out the snob, keep out the cad,
And all impurity and sin,
But let the tired and patient in.

Shams, pomps, pain, the Devil
Himself, and all his imps of evil,
If they should dare to prowl about,
Put up thy bar, and keep them out.

And when some day, with solemn face,
Winged Azrael shall cleave through space,
Hither to bear my soul away,
Usher him in without delay.

The Reverend John Carmichael was pastor of the Forks of Brandywine Presbyterian Church. The title of the following poem has not been included, but it is Blanche Nevin's poem about her maternal great-grandfather's Revolutionary War activities.

Carmicheal, great grand daddy of mine,
Was Scottish of blood, of the Argyle line.
His sermons were dull, but his soul was fine

Washington's soldiers at Valley Forge,
Huddled together, defied King George.
Wounded and fevered, their chill-blained toes
Wrapped in rags, they hungered and froze.

Bold in his pulpit Carmichael outspoke;
"England is tyrannous. Throw off the yoke.
Smite the oppressor. God giveth the right
Of freedom to all men. Go forward and fight."

Washington wrote him, "Full sorely we need
Bandages, liniments, all things, indeed.
Homesick and heartsick, the men in despair
Long for your sympathy comfort and care."

Carmichale mounted his horse, and he rode
From farmer to farmer, to every abode,
Crying out to his people: "Give all that ye can;
Scrape from your penury, woman and man."

But the women cried: "Dominie, what can we do?
We've given already our utmost to you;
Of linen, of homespun, we're almost bereft.
God help us? We've only our petticoats left."

"Shorten your petticoats. Cut from them bands;

Make lint of your rags with industrious hands;
Crowd ye my sallle bags, off will I ride
And carry your bounty to Washington's side."

And Carmichael took them, for hourses were few—
His only was left, when our army passed through;
"For the Dominie needed his horse," they said,
"To visit the sick and bury the dead."

So to and fro went he from valley to camp,
In peril of spy and of treacherous scamp.
The British at once put a price on his head;
"Capture him living, or capture him dead."

"Catch Carmichael wherever he goes.
He is one of his majesty's dangerous foes.
Plug him with bullets, with bayonet ram him.
He is helping his majesty's enemies—damn him."
The night was silent, the night was dark—
All were asleep in the manse—when hark!
There comes a clatter of galloping speed,
There comes a courier lashing his steed.

Under the window the messenger cries:
"Wake, Carmichael. Carmichael arise.
There is rumor tonight of a British advance;
Washington bids you to take no chance."

"If you don't hurry, you forfeit your head;
Linger no longer, but out of your bed,
Off to the forests, and do not delay;
Up to your saddle, and off and away."

"Ford the Brandywine. Fly for your life;
Take your daughter and take your wife

Deep in the forests, and there abide,
In the tents of red men safely hide."

There was nothing to do but fly. They fled.
When in jeopardy, do not lose your head.
Two on the horse, and the rest in a cart,
With the family silver and salt, they start.

For at that time salt was hoarded with care;
None could be bought. It was precious and rare.
But fording the water, alack a day!
The salt got wet and melted away.

There is no record of what they did,
Where they went or how they hid.
But war was over they soon came back,
Horse and cart and an empty sack.
Yes! War was over. We grounded our arms.
And the worn-out soldiers returned to their farms.
Theirs was the sacrifice, suffering, pain;
Ours is liberty, profit and gain.

See to it, ye who listen to me,
With ears to hear, and eyes to see,
That a heritage purchased at such a cost,
By fraud or chicanery never be lost.

Dominie Carmichael died in his bed,
And in spite of the price that was put on his head,
His skull was still attached to his spine,
When they buried that great grand daddy of mine.

This was written during President Theodore Roosevelt's presidency.
She sculpted a bust of "Teddy," but its location is not known.

"The bi-centennial celebration of the first settlement made in Lancaster County was held at the Willow Street Mennonite church on Thursday, September 8. One part of the program rendered is of special interest to the people of this locality, a poem by Miss Blanche Nevin, of Churchtown. Blanche's play with words has been understood by some as 'Ode to the Pennsylvania Dutch.' The poem is entitled '"Owed" to the Lancaster Dutch,' and was received with much applause from all. The poem follows:"

(This quote, preceding "'Owed' To The Lancaster Dutch," was found without a reference to the source, a newspaper clipping.)

"OWED" TO THE
LANCASTER DUTCH

First
Hurrah for the Lancaster Dutch!
    To earn us our bread,
    He goes early to bed,
And rises while yet it is dark
He anticipates even the lark
    He milks all the cows,
    He plants and he plows.
That a sleepy old world may be fed.
    Hurrah for the Lancaster Dutch,
    Our Country's reliable crutch.
He has wheat, he has corn, he has oats,
He has horses and cows, he has shoats,
Geese, turkeys and chickens to pluck;
And a baby each year, "if in luck,"
He deserves every cent in his hutch.
Hurrah for the Lancaster Dutch.
The wife of the Lancaster Dutch
With suffragettes isn't in touch,
    Her vinegar kegs

Her butter and eggs
Attention absorb overmuch.

Second

She hardly can heed
Roosevelt's praises indeed
Nor compliment bothers to read,
    She stews and she fries,
    She makes punkin pies,
    She shines pot and pan,
    She darns for her man;
She sews and she knits,
Dried cherries and snitz,
With pretty brown eyes
Each crevice she tries
To sweep and to scrub everys-mutch.
    She bakes
    And she makes
    Griddle cakes.
And sausage, and paunhous, and sauer-kraut.
And doughnuts, sweitzer, noodle soup, scrapple
And sweifleish, and stink case, and dumplings of
apple.
    Huh! The wife of the Lancaster Dutch
    Don't trouble with politics much
    Heaven grant her hereafter a wreath,
    And in this world—the best of store teeth.

Third

At last when "the farms" they resign,
And go up on their "Hook and Hair line."
Their mansion in Heaven to enter
Their Amish and Mennonite center,
The shutters they close here so tight,

90

Will open to fresh air and light.
And shining white robes they will wear,
Without hooks or buttons up there.
They will not have to wait
Very long at the gate.
As may be your lot, or my own.
When we seek the eternal bright throne.
For truly our Lord understands
The religion of labor-worn hands,
Of eloquent noble worn hands,
Which the Fisherman Peter will clutch
To welcome the Lancaster Dutch.

Blanche Nevin
Windsor Forges, September 7, between 1901-1909

Blanche's sense of humor in everyday events is seen in this short poem. It appears she may have had some familiarity with the problem.

THE IMP SCIATICA

I am Sciatica! I've got the nerve—
   I never hesitate, if I observe
Nice men and women sitting at their ease—
   I pounce upon them, and I twist their knees.

I am Sciatica! I tumble down
   The haughty tyrant and the humble clown,
The holiest man you ever saw will slip
   If I can catch him once upon the hip

Blanche initially wrote "Jessie Come In" on the occasion of Jessie Wilson and Francis Sayre meeting at Windsor Forge on his Easter break. Some years later, at the Lancaster County Historical Society annual outing to Elizabeth Farms and Furnace on July 11, 1913, Blanche sang this poem to the assemblage. The young couple's engagement had recently been announced (Vol. 17, 15). This was when it was given the title, "Bridal Welcome Song."

BRIDAL WELCOME SONG
By Miss Blanche Nevin

The following song was dedicated to Miss Jessie Wilson, daughter of President Wilson. The words were set to music by Miss Nevin as a welcome to Miss Jessie into the Nevin family.

> Fling the door open, and swing the gate wide,
> Welcome the entering feet of the bride.
> Eager the groom at the threshold stands.
> Holding his arms, and his outstretched hands.
> Blessed are you who true love win!
> > Jessie, come in—
> > > Come in.

> In heat of summer, in winter's cold,
> This roof shall shelter you, young or old;
> Come weal, come woe, whate'er betide;
> Palm to palm, and side by side,
> Into the house of your true love's kin,
> > Jessie come in—
> > > Come in.

> Sweet pink clover, bloom over the grass,
> Welcome the lover here with his lass,
> Bride of the golden hair and eyes
> Blue with the luminous hue of the skies,
> Blessed are you who true love win!
> > Jessie, come in—
> > > Come in.

In Volume 21, Lancaster County Historical Society preserved the poem Blanche Nevin wrote and read at the dedication of the George Ross Historical Marker, June 4, 1897—all thirty-three verses.

She re-read the poem in the Iris Club rooms, (1896-97, January meeting) a reading full of fire and fervor, of the days of 1776.[25]

MISS BLANCHE NEVIN'S POEM

The following is the exquisite gem read by Miss Blanche Nevin. As will be seen, it rehearses the story of the events preceding and leading up to the Declaration of Independence, and pays a glowing tribute to the fifty-six "good men and true" who affixed their names to that immortal paper.

I.

To chafing hearts in sorest need,
To people fretting to be freed
From foreign yoke, when foreign greed
        With taxes wrung them;
God gave strong leaders, not a few,
Courageous men, upright and true,
And—Lancaster—He gave to you
        George Ross among them.

II.

Ill brooked the sons of pioneers
The sound of cowardice, and sneers
From dapper soldiery in his ears.
        It was small wonder,
Defiance was hurled back again
By irritated frontiersmen;
To tease the wild wolves in their den
        Was fatal blunder.

III.

(Ah! after many a bitter year
Each braggart boast and swaggering jeer
Cost every pretty soldier dear
    As they surrendered.
When beaten, and with downcast head,
Their hats pulled low, and eyelids red,
They followed in Cornwallis' tread,
    As swords were tendered.)

IV.

Long time it was the writhing land
Insulted felt the tyrant hand
The spark was waiting to be fanned
    On freedom's altar.
Yet, though the cause be just and right,
Long will men hesitate to fight,
If "round their necks is pressing tight
    A threatened halter."

V.

But yet we know—dear Liberty—
Man is about as true to thee
As, with his nature, he can be
    To any woman;
That very neck for thy sweet sake
At certain times he risks to break;
Nor holds his life too dear to stake,
    Nor all things human.

VI.

And Patrick Henry's passionate breath,
"Oh, give me liberty or death,"
Thrilled through the anxious land beneath

All party faction.
Throughout the broad Atlantic States
Where brooding war, impatient, waits
The moment which precipitates
    The crash of action.

VII.

And so, when time was ripe, men came
From far and near to sign each name
Upon that proudest roll of fame,
    Our Declaration.
Facing disgrace, that patriot band,
The nervous force of all the land,
Stretched out the pen and sinewy hand
    That framed the nation.

VIII.

Now let the British lion lash
With angry tails her sides, and gnash
Her teeth and bounding forward dash
    With roaring hollow!
At last the eagle's wings have grown,
The chain is snapped which held him down;
High in the air when he was flown,
    Lions can't follow!

IV.

Good faith! That day you need not think
That Philadelphia lacked for ink;
Or men, whose fingers did not shrink
    At thought of fetters.
For well each knew that shortest shrift,
And tightest rope, and highest lift,
Might be to him stern England's gift
    For those few letters.

X.

Aye—every signer knew that war
Would follow and torment him sore.
Outlawed by it—and all his store
    Unless he hid it—
Was forfeit to the distant king.
Who held him but a chattel thing
From which another tax to wring,
    And yet—he did it.

XI.

Men made for the occasion, they,
More apt for earnest work than play.
Coined for the purpose of the day,
    From precious metal
Men to a solemn epoch sent,
Shaped by the friction of event
To fitness for some great intent,
    New thoughts to settle.

XII.

Men of big frame and bigger heart
Which had not lost the power to smart
Of pious faith—the greater part
    Of training holy.
Who yet felt heaven in sun and sky,
And held themselves when they should die
Responsible to God on high,
    And to God solely.

XIII.

Who dreaded an avenging hell,
And honor prized too dear to sell,
Who did not love their lives too well

To risk for others.
For a great principle of right
Willing to die, ready to fight,
Who kept their conscience clean and bright,
    And loved their brothers.

XIV.

Doubtless before his lot was cast,
Each hero struggled through a past
Of dubious fears, but, at the last,
    All vacillation
And tremor being thrust aside,
Purpose was resolute, to abide
Whatever upshot should betide
    The new-fledged nation.

XV.

Fifty-six names were written there,
In all the world's long history, where
Find ye a list which can compare
    With this in glory? Of nobler lives; of fairer
fames;
Of less self-interested aims;
Of cleaner, more untarnished names,
    There is no story.

XVI.

First, Massachusetts, stung to rage
By foolish North or fatuous Gage,
Sent five strong men to sign the page,
    From different classes.
And Hancock, gentleman, indeed,
Wrote down his name to take the lead;
"So large," he said, "the king may read
    Mine without glasses."

XVII.

Adams, the incorruptible!
Who "loved the public good too well
For private gain its rights to sell,"
    Noble in scorning.
Whose voice with no uncertain ring,
When agents came a bribe to bring.
Sent back that message to the king
    and "gave him warning."

XVII.

Impetuous Houston, in his race
For Zubley, lost deserved place
Among the founders of his race.
    Subley, a spying
Judas, discovered in the act
Of treachery, denied the fact,
But fled to Georgia; Houston tracked
    The traitor flying.

XIX.

And frequent was the moment, when
The casting vote which made free men
Was given by the State of Penn,
    Amid confusion.
For Morton, to our lasting pride,
Came forward when the vote was tied,
And cast his ballot on the side
    Of revolution.

XX.

Carroll—(lest people would not know)—
Added "of Carrollton" to show
Which Carroll faced the dangerous foe,
    "Now hang together

Or we'll hang separately," said he.
The die was cast, and valiantly
And long they faced a stormy sea
    Ere cleared the weather.

XXI.

We glean from the recording pen
Truth which is now, was also then,
Conspicuous—that heroic men
    Had noble mothers.
And Francis Lewis—(kindly grant
Attention to my modest vaunt)
Was "brought up by his maiden aunt,"
    And "there are others."

XXII.

The more one hears—the more one reads,
Examining their lives and deeds,
The more the critic spirit heeds
    With admiration.
Ere half their worthiness was sung,
If praises due should well be rung,
Your ears would weary of my tongue
    And its narration.

XXIII.

Among the strongest and the best
Our delegate sustained the test,
And cast his ballot with the rest.
    Brave, wise and witty,
Of broad, well educated mind;
King's advocate, and well inclined
To weigh the rights of human kind,
    Ross, of our city!

XXIV.

To-day we come, with honest pride,
From city and from country side,
To mark the spot where did abide
    This man of merit.
And make the letters deep and clean
That they may last for many a year,
To testify that we hold dear
    What we inherit.

XXV.

It is not meet that gratitude,
Or loving memory of the good.
Should perish—for the coffin wood
    Can only cover
The dust—the vehicle of clay,
Which served the soul its passing day,
The deeds of men die not away,
    Are never over.

XXVI.

The world was better where he trod,
When George Ross rendered up to God
His soul—his body to the sod,
    Well done his duty.
The white man and the red man, too,
Full well his generous justice knew.
Bright his example shines for you,
    A thing of beauty.

XXVII.

Our town, recognizant of zeal,
And service for the common weal,
Voted him "costly plate," "genteel
    And ornamented."

But he the civic gift put by
Making magnanimous reply,
"Only what each should do did I!"
  Modest—contented.

XXVIII.

We offer to his memory's sake,
The gift he, living, would not take;
And tribute of affection make
  With hearty pleasure.
God rest his soul, where'er it be,
Safe in the peace which such as he
Deserve throughout eternity,
  In goodly measure.

XXIX.

The story of the war is fraught
With lesson, and renews the thought
That nothing great was ever wrought
  Without hard trial.
Gold cannot buy, beyond dispute,
God's highest gifts. The finest fruit
And flower of goodness take their root,
  In self-denial.

XXX.

Lancastrians, who your acres plough,
Whose fertile fields are ripening now,
In gratitude, remember how
  They were defended.
What years of suffering were borne,
How long the sharpened sword was worn;
How great the hunger, scant the corn,
  Ere war was ended.

XXXI.

See ye to it—who peacefully stand
And gather with unshackled hand
The crops that ripen in the land
    In generous bounty;
See ye to it that not in vain
Their red blood soaked the battle plain,
When men for liberty were slain,
    Oh, town and county!

XXXII.

The present guardians of your race
A little while ye fill a space,
Rise to the duties of your place!
    If care relaxes,
New forms of tyranny creep in;
Greed and corruption will begin,
Be vigilant, or they will win.
    Look to your taxes!

XXXIII.

Stand by your colors without fear,
In spite of cynic, scoff and jeer,
See that you treat "Old Glory" dear
    With reverent manner.
God help the day—God help the hour
If hearts degenerate lose the power
To thrill—to glow at sight of our
    Star Spangled Banner

BLANCHE NEVIN
Lancaster, June 4th, 1897

This poem, "Maud Muller," was the stimulus for Blanche's bust, Maud Muller, of marble which was shown at both Philadelphia Centennial Exposition (1876) and the Chicago World Exposition (1893).

In Chicago it was placed in the Hall of Honor, Women's Pavilion. It is thought to be the bust now in the Iris Club rooms, given by William Hager. His father, John Hager was familiar with Blanche's work since he served on the first art commission of Pennsylvania. That commission selected Blanche for the Muhlenberg statue. The committee gave the sculptors, Blanche and Howard Roberts, their subjects, Robert Fulton and Muhlenberg, for Statuary Hall, D.C.

This is the only poem in this book not written by Blanche Nevin.

MAUD MULLER
John Greenleaf Whittier[50]

The recollection of some descendants of a Hessian deserter in the Revolutionary war bearing the name of Muller doubtless suggested the somewhat infelicitous title of a New England idyll. The poem had no real foundation in fact, though a hint of it may have been found in recalling an incident, trivial in itself, of a journey on a picturesque Maine seaboard with my sister some years before it was written. We had stopped to rest our tired horse under the shade of an apple-tree, and refresh him with water from a little brook which rippled through the stone wall across the road. A very beautiful young girl in scantest summer attire was at work in the hayfield, and as we talked with her we noticed that she strove to hide her bare feet by raking hay over them blushing as she did so, through the tan of her cheek and neck.

MAUD MULLER
by John Greenleaf Whittier, 1845

Maud Muller on a summer's day,
Raked the meadow sweet with hay.

Beneath her torn hat glowed the wealth
Of simple beauty and rustic health.

Singing, she wrought, and her merry glee
The mock-bird echoed from this tree.

But when she glanced to the far-off town,
White from its hill-slope looking down,

The sweet song died, and a vague unrest
And a nameless longing filled her breast,

A wish, that she hardly dared to own,
For something better than she had known.

The Judge rode slowly down the lane,
Smoothing his horse's chestnut mane.

He drew his bridle in the shade
Of the apple-trees, to greet the maid,

And asked a draught from the spring that flowed
Through the meadow across the road.

She stooped where the cool spring bubbled up,
And filled for him her small tin cup,

And blushed as she gave it, looking down

On her feet so bare, and her tattered gown.

"Thanks!" said the Judge; "a sweeter draught
From a fairer hand was never quaffed."

He spoke of the grass and flowers and trees,
Of the singing birds and the humming bees;

Then talked of the haying, and wondered whether
The cloud in the west would bring foul weather.

And Maud forgot her brier-torn gown,
And her graceful ankles bare and brown;

And listened, while a pleased surprise
Looked from her long-lashed hazel eyes.

At last, like one who for delay
Seeks a vain excuse, he rode away.

Maud Muller looked and sighed: "Ah me!
That I the Judge's bride might be!

"He would dress me up in silks so fine,
And praise and toast me at his wine.

"My father should wear a broadcloth coat;
My brother should sail a painted boat.

"I'd dress my mother so grand and gay,
And the baby should have a new toy each day.

"And I'd feed the hungry and clothe the poor,
And all should bless me who left our door."

The Judge looked back as he climbed the hill,
And saw Maud Muller standing still.

And sweet Maud Muller's hazel eyes
Looked out in their innocent surprise.

Oft, when the wine in his glass was red,
He longed for the wayside well instead;

And close his eyes on his garnished rooms
To dream of meadows and clover-blooms.

And the proud man sighed, with a secret pain,
"Ah, that I were free again!

"Free as when I rode that day,
Where the barefoot maiden raked her hay."

She wedded a man unlearned and poor,
And many children played round her door.

But care and sorrow, and childbirth pain,
Left their traces on heart and brain.

And oft, when the summer sun shone hot
On the new-mown hay in the meadow lot,

And she heard the little spring brook fall
Over the roadside, through the wall,

In the shade of the apple-tree again
She saw a rider draw his rein.

And, gazing down with timid grace,

She felt his pleased eyes read her face.
"A form more fair, a face more sweet,
Ne'er hath it been my lot to meet.

"And her modest answer and graceful air
Show her wise and good as she is fair.

"Would she were mine, and I to-day,
Like her, a harvester of hay;

"No doubtful balance of rights and wrongs,
Nor weary lawyers with endless tongues,

"But low cattle and song of birds,
And health and quiet and loving words."

But he thought of his sisters, proud and cold,
And his mother, vain of her rank and gold.

So, closing his heart, the Judge rode on,
And Maud was left in the field alone.

But the lawyers smiled that afternoon,
When he hummed in court an old love-tune;

And the young girl mused beside the well
Till the rain on the unraked clover fell.

He wedded a wife of richest dower,
Who loved for fashion, as he for power.

Yet oft, in his marble hearth's bright glow,
He watched a picture come and go;

Sometimes her narrow kitchen walls
Stretched away into stately halls;

The weary wheel to a spinnet turned,
The tallow candle an astral burned,

And for him who sat by the chimney lug,
Dozing and grumbling o'er pipe and mug,

A manly form at her side she saw,
And joy was duty and love was law.

Then she took up her burden of life again,
Saying only, "It might have been."

Alas for maiden, alas for Judge,
For rich repiner and household drudge!

God pity them both! and pity us all,
Who vainly the dreams of youth recall.

For of all sad words of tongue or pen,
The saddest are these: "It might have been!"

Ah, well! for us all some sweet hope lies
Deeply buried from human eyes;

And, in the hereafter, angels may
Roll the stone from its grave away!

The poems you have just read were found in several places as noted in the bibliography by the author. The remainder are poems copied from the originals, some in handwriting, some typed by her nephews, John Nevin Sayre and Francis Bowes Sayre. Faith Sayre Schindler (Mrs. George), a grandniece of Blanche, graciously allowed the poems to be copied for publication. Coming late in the research, they will add to the poetic legacy of Blanche Nevin. You will see that she wrote poems while she travelled all around the world as well as in summers at the seashore.

NEW YEAR 1881

Comest thou hither as friend or as foe, New Year?
Icy and glittering, mantelled in snow New Year?
What do you bear in the pack on your back New Year?
Births, and marriages, murders? Alack, New Year
Each will get what he did not expect New Year
Some will be glorified, some will be wretched, New Year
Coming in rudeness or coming in grace, New Year
I snap my fingers and laugh in your face!

UNTITLED

No more to fly on free expanded wing
Low at my feet thou liest dead poor thing.

Alas! Too late do I repent the haste
Which doomed thy beauty to such tragic waste.

Not all our boasted science can restore
Thee, perfect bird, destroyed forevermore
The air doth dissipate thy parting ghost
This world is poorer of thy presence lost

No more glittering sunlight shines for thee
No more the fresh brine foams upon the sea

Nature regretting chants thy funeral dirge
Down where the winds and waves of ocean surge

I can but hope that on no brooding nest,
Smoothing the ruffled feathers of her breast

No other bird lamenting long and late
The tardy coming of his recreant mate

Awaits in vain the music of his flight
Throughout the troubled watches of the night

SPRING

Spring — Spring
Lazy, dawdling thing!
Waken, arise,
And rub your eyes
Who ___
    If not you
Will chase the snow away
    O' Day?

Lift
Each muddy drift
Shake this misty atmosphere
Make it warm and clear
Spring, Spring,
Dilatory thing,
Come and do your duty
Fill the land with beauty
To this damp world of ours
Bring fragrance and flowers
Bring birds
    And make them sing,
Please, Spring

GOODBYE HOOP SKIRT

I

Dropt by my hand this minute from my waist
There on the floor in circling coils, ye lie
My hoops, dear hoops, which oft my toilette graced
I bid you now a sorrowful goodbye.
No more will ye my silken robe uphold
From dirty streets or loathed tobacco dye,
Alas! My gown must fall in shrunken fold
And trail, since hoops are out of fashion I am told.

II

Where first our petticoats ye did expand
How well remembered the distant hour,
Father and brothers, an opposing band,
At thy proportions dubiously did lower,
While some made fun of ye and some looked sour
The daily papers too raised quite a storm
Yet over all the triumphant was your power
And o'er our critics too when they waxed warm
Pronouncing ye of inartistic form.

III

Fashion commanded and we trod the street
Steel clad as were wandering knights of old
T'was pleasant save when snarling about our feet
Some puny dog than other dogs more bold
Would creep beneath your petticoats broad fold
And there, still snarling, put us in such fright
Lest as around our gaitered feet he rolled
He might our trembling toes and ankles bite
Yet this at very worst was only a rare plight.

III

Each day your comfort more conspicuous grew,
Defects ye covered, often grace supplied
Without ye what will poor Matilda do

While Kate, a perfect giantress will stride
Now when two ladies linger side by side
One will be thin when we thought plump before,
The other will be dumpy, round and wide.
Yet fashion bid us wear hoops no more
We sigh and sighing leave ye dropt upon the floor.

THE GARRET

As o'er the old homestead my footsteps I bend
In each room, in each chimney beholding a friend
The stairs that I stood on with heedless young feet,
Which time has controlled to a measure more meet,
The window whence off o'er the sunny glass green
glass
I watched with young eyes the dark cloud shadows
pasts,
And gazed beyond where the mountains lie
And thought Parnells Knob* was touching the sky
Oh the rooms, and the stairs, and the windows were
dead,
And they soften my heart as their faces appear.
Yet I mount the old stairs soon after passing the hall
For the dear dear old garret is loved more than all
O garret, old garret the time has been long
Since your rafters heard my noisiest song
O garret, old garret, my heart has been sore
And I don't sing as much as I used to of yore
And don't you remember how often I fled
When weeping to hide in your corners my head;
Since then o'er that head have passed merciful years
Yet o'er the same cheeks sometimes glide the old
tears.
For I'm what men call sensitive just as of old
And God help me sometimes—hearts are so cold.
And when crushed from my soul the
      wine drops of sorrow will fall
I have longed for your shelter best loved of all.
You're the same just as ever, the very old stains,
Every nail, every shingle, and rafter remains,
I could fancy the cobwebs that swing in the air,
Are the very same cobwebs that used to be there.

I used to dread spooks, but now gladly I see,
The ghosts of the past cluster closely round me,
And o'er me their blessing seems softly to fall,
For I loved this old garret most dearly of all.

---

*Parnell's Knob is a distinct knob, away from the eastern base of Tucaroras Mountain, and is visible to residents of Mercersburg. Old Route 30 went by its base in Franklin County, Pennsylvania. Parnell's Restuarant was known around the state for its country ham meals.

UNTITLED

Listen Hark! Azrael sings
Time to go—put on thy rings

Onward to the chrystal star
Where the radiant angels are
Where the fragrant violet smells
And the purple saphodelles

Slip thy chrysalis and fly
Irridescent butterfly
Clearance a high exultant way
Unbeclogged by hindering clay

See an ecstacy of light
Meander through in the infinite
Eyes can see and ears can hear
In celestial atmosphere.

Heart, whose banishment is past
Merge thyself in God at last.

Listen, Hark, Azrael sings
Time to go—put on your wings.
(1918)

UNTITLED

On the banks of the ____ they are crowded
Battered, brushriven, unshrouded
Oh Cherubs get ready, get ready
To row your boat stalwart and steady

Out of the festering trenches
Reeking with poisonous stenches
The death rigor hardly erases
The hate and despair in their faces

Row them across the deep river
Flowing black tide and deliver
Them up at the uttermost border
To the arms of the angel recorder

Their cycle of this world is rounded
They enter our regions unshrouded
Infinity's sphere is before them
Eternity's atmosphere awaits them.

They return nevermore here beside us
The blasts and the darkness divide us
The voice of our weeping they heed not
Our love and devotion they need not.

CONGE 1878-1879

Let us give him a bumper for memories sake
Parting always is better and makes the headache
He has been to us treacherous—treated us badly
Unattached how anxious to bid it adieu
And be off with the old love and on with the new

So give him a bumper, then sentiment smother
And jilt him tonight as we welcome another
The act is ungracious, this having to hurt him
But indeed he deserves it—the lesson would hurt him
And don't call it fickle, or false, or untrue
So be off with the old love and on with the new

For age is progressive so onward we go
We aspire we improve, we develop, we grow
And very few people of true worth sustain
From year's end, and year's end exactly the same.
Higher nature demands higher sympathy too
So—off with the old love and on with the new

Then sometimes old love is exacting and jealous
Is careless of pleasing and not over zealous
We discovered our faults and unless superhuman
Admits the attraction of some other woman
Our face is no longer enough for his view
So off with the old and on with the new.

In faultless old love there is grief and despair
But new love—Ah—new love is brilliant and fair!
Carries hope in his countenance, promises brightly
Hides away every possible sorrow politely
Let us trust in him recklessly, fickle or true
And be off with the old love and on with the new.

HOW TO DRESS TOMATOES

Do it yourself, a servant's taste's too rough,
They season over much, or not enough.
Nice hands are needed, and artistic skill
If you, to blend the compounds *finely* will.
An apron large put well your dress about
For juice *will* squirt and yellow seeds fly out
Then don't get hurried, if you fail, don't fret
And try, not one ingredient to forget.

The smooth tomato is the best to choose
Though crooked *large* ones rarely I refuse
But they are troublesome to nicely skin
The _____ sides do stick so deeply in
Best take those fleshy round ones which appear
To tempt you with their surface polished clear
Then having skinned them, through the veiny side
Let your bold knife with reckless _____ glide
Yet tear as well as cut _____ in stiff round
But tempting tidbits let the dish abound
Nor yet too small let these same morsels be
But large enough to let the seeds go free.
Yes "gouge" the seeds and all the juice you can
With ease express, drain gently from your pan
Then o'er them put a scattering of salt
Too little is I think the usual fault
But taste and practice only, will combine
To make you quite an adept in this line
Tastes are so various too you rarely find
In this respect two families of one mind
"De gustibus non disputaredemus est"
Is very true and happily expressed.

So far so good but better further on

For now you must consider all you've done
Only a preparation for the rest
And yet a preparation that gives zest
Somehow or other to the finished dish
A lucious look and colour crimsonish
A half a teaspoonful of mustard take
With slippery oil its fiery dryness slake
If rightly mingled they will well _____
Then with your spoon soft-rubbing add the bright
The golden globe that in the boiled egg lies
Until the three shall fairly harmonize
Now slice a half an onion very fine
(This is the taste of others, none of mine)
And _____ pretty parsley leaves cut up
Without regretful sigh for man must sup
Nor stop to mourn the beauty that he eats
For nobody wants bitters with their sweets
So cut the pretty parsley leaves and then
Take up the white part of the egg again
Slice it too nicely then with it combined
Add two small peppers of the sharpest kind
To smallest morsels cut, then o'er the whole
At last assembled in a little bowl
Onion and peppers, parsley egg and all
Pour the sour juice which vinegar one call

Again drain off the water from the fruit
Place in whatever wish dish you have to suit
I like it on white china much the best
The contrast thrown out is the prettiest
Pour on your dressing now and you will find
A dish I think well suited to your mind
Only a little taste of it would make
A cannibal his usual food forsake

UNTITLED

[May have been expressing her grief
at her father's death]
Underneath the damp mould we laid him down to
rest,
With the white Calla lillies lying on his breast;
Lying on his breast and around about his head;
White were the Calla lillies, white the soul that fled.

Heavy fell the damp mould on the coffin lid,
Still face and Calla lillies underneath were hid.
Heavy when the prayer was said our heart turned
away
Nevermore to see him till the resurrection day.

Nevermore to look on the face to us so dear,
Oh Christ! It will be very weary waiting here,
Heed the aching of our hearts—hear us while we
pray
For the dawn of the morn of the resurrection day.

COLUMBUS

"Is he dead yet?"
   Mark Twain in *Innocents Abroad*
Written on day of Columbian celebration, New York

Do you hear what the drums say? Hark!
Oh no, he is not dead yet, Mark.

Oh no, he is not dead
   You can listen to his feet,
For to day I heard his tread
   With the people on the street.
He stood, the oldest resident
   To day at City Hall
Mid Cabinet and President
   Most vital of them all.

Oh no, Mark, he is not dead at all
To night he intends to give a ball
He will dance with the ladies at the ball.
Do you hear what the drums say? Hark!
Oh Columbus isn't dead yet, —Mark!

"E DOLCE FAR NIENTE"

E dolce far Niente. Let my boat glide
Down with the current, onward with the tide
Floating into sunshine, into shadow tossed
Nerveless my arms, my oars before me crossed
      E dolce far Niente.

All the hot morning in the desperate strife
Spending at noon the swooning force of life
Now the work is done, now the day is spent
Idle and in silence let me float content
      E dolce far Niente.

Ah, if one was sure effort was the best
Wiser than this floating, braver than this rest
If our rowing brought us into nobler seas
We might welcome struggle, spurn in glorious ease,
      E dolce far Niente.

But the forceful current of resistless fate
Him who steers against it, crushes soon or late
When we strive against it, strive to stem the flood
Doing may be marring of the highest good
      E dolce far Niente.

To the weary eyes dulled by toil and care
Come no sight of beauty where true beauties are
Heaven is not so blue, earth is not so sweet
They are not the blossoms scattered at their feet.
      E dolce far Niente.

E dolce far Niente onward little boat
E dolce far Niente, aimless will I float,
Into the vast wilderness, out of the glaring light
On to the quiet stars—into the purple night.
      E dolce far Niente.

THE BIRD THAT SINGS IN THE RAIN

Part 1.

The roses, I am not denying
That bloom in the sunshiny days
Are very commendable, trying
Their best, and deserving of praise.

And so is our Peggy, who daily
Goes forth when the sunny days glow,
Bedecked in a pretty, frock, gaily
Rejoicing the eyes of her beaux;

And so are the apples, the cherries,
The ripening plum, and the peach,
Which mellow in sunshine, and berries
Are good, and industrious each.

I honor each one for the pleasure
They give us again and again,
But respect without stint, beyond measure
The Bird that can sing in the rain.

The week has been muggy unduly,
It rained every night and each day;
And Peggy droops languid and bluely
In a dingy old garment of grey.

Allow undisturbed this reflection,
That Nature has marvellous ways,
Whose defects far surpass our perfections,
Whose blunders much challenge our praise.

While we can be joyful or tearful
At will, and are able to change,

The Rain-bird is bound to be cheerful
By law of its organic range.

Unbothererd by subtle selection,
Unchecked by a wherefore or why,
Fulfilling its beings direction
It must give out music or die.

To make it to duty decided
Was needed some excellent plan
Therefore a defect was provided
To make it more faithful—than *man,*

Who, otherwise excellent being
Is apt to be fickle and light;
Oh, why did not Nature, forseeing
Continue her policy bright

And force him to duty, preventing
That volatile fancy should stray
It would save us a lot of lamenting
If his heart was constructed that way.

Part 2.
Thus far had I written concerning
This subject, when, chatty and gay
Came Julia, who, bristling with learning
Remarked in a casual way,

"Have you noticed a bird when it's raining,
Pour forth a melliferous note?
It would die if it did not, the straining
Of dampness so presses its throat."
Then I cried, "Oh, my erudite neighbor

I fear we shall certainly quarrel
If you come thus and ruin my labor
By spoiling the point of my moral!

Alas, I have not been to college
To study construction of birds;
And now you come in with your knowledge
And shatter the sense of my words.

Yet I am not the first whose conclusion
Was founded on premises wrong,
For often cold fact works confusion
In well built up science or song.

And so I will rally—and gather
New thought from this curious thing,
That not its will power, but the weather
Compells this bit creature to sing.

She mopes on the sofa, and dozes;
All Nature looks stupid outside,
Bedraggled, discolored, the roses
Have lost every vestage of pride.

The garden is sodden and dreary,
Exhausted each topic of talk,
And pent in the house until weary
Nobody goes out for a walk.

But out on the cold sulky morning,
Through clouds that were hopelessly grey
The song of a bird, without warning,
Saluted the coming of day.
And joyous his note and right royal

His faith, optimistic and good;
Obedient to duty and loyal
To Nature whatever her mood.

From your pulpit of oak, tiny teacher,
You carroll your sermon of hope,
Of courage, of patience, a preacher.
More powerful than bishop or pope.

When nothing at all is the matter
When brilliant and cloudless the sky
We all can be cheerful and chatter,
And no one is brighter than I.

If, by some judicious provision,
He had to be faithful perforce,
Was lacking the power of decision,
Was good, as a matter of course.

Just fancy, at once the cessation,
Of cause for indefinite strife!
What a change in each human relation
What agreeable change—to his wife!

So, Julia my dear, moralizing
I've studied a lesson again;
How much can be learned is surprising
From birds that sing out in the rain.

But when the blue skies are beclouded,
Like Peggy, I fail to be gay,
When the warm sun is hidden, and shrouded,
I lack your superior way.
Oh, creature of fluff and of feather,

And fragile allotment of wing,
Regardless of dark stormy weather
You perch above trouble and sing.

So I "Take off my hat" as I follow
Your clear and electric refrain,
And own that you "beat me all hollow,"
Sweet bird that can sing in the rain.

NATURE AND THE HYPOCRITE
A VISION

On the world's edge—gazing with awe—
As the dense mists unrolled, this I saw.

One who on earth had rendered up his breath
And shed his body at the bed of death,
Came where the angel of the judgement stood,
Taking the testimony of all good
And evil deeds.
Him no one can deceive.
With him nor he avails, nor makes believe.
He draweth all hid sweetness forth at last;
And comforts goodness for its sorrows past.

To him approaching came the newly dead,
And "Give me Heaven, condemn me not, he pled"
"See thou my blameless life? No human eye
One blot on my clean record can descry.
The world lamenteth me with honeyed praise
And crowned the memory of my vanished days.
There is none witnesseth against me.
None hath seen aught evil that my hand hath done."

Then from innumerable stars rang out
Voices from purple depths, a mighty shout

"Against thy soul as witnesses we rise;
We saw thee sin. We watched thee from the skies.

Then came there thither, borne upon the blast,
Leaves of the forest—myriads, hurrying eddying fast.
"We—we are thine accusers, who did see
Thy crime, and come to witness against thee,"

Circling the chattering flocks of birds flew in
"We testify against thee and thy sin;
With every forest leaf and glittering star
We bearing witness thine accusers are."

Thereat that hypocrite turned him about
Self-judged and screamed "My sin hath found me out
And crying "Hide me and receive me Hell"
Plunged into space and fell—, fell—, fell—.

MY WATCH AT GINEVA

"We must part my watch," said I,
"We must part to day
You are false and won't keep time
So the jewelers say."

"Tick, tick, tick," my watch it spoke
"Tick, tick, tick," each word
I bent my ear to where it lay
And this is what I heard.

Ah, is it true that we must part
Must we really sever?
I who've been so near your heart
And hoped to stay forever?

In your gown my face I hid,
Yet though out of sight,
With my little hands I toiled
For you day and night.

All your secrets I know well
And before I stop
Don't you fear that I may tell
In the jewelers shop?

"Don't you fear that I may say
Why your heart beats quick?
I know how it went that day
When you were—tick, tick, tick."

Here I quickly raised my head
On the table bowed,

"Tattletale hush up," I said
"Do not tick so loud."

"Yes we have been nearest friends,
What you say is true,
I've consulted none more oft,
Than I've consulted you.

I've a certain fondness too
For your little face
Grown familiar—yet you are
Justly in disgrace.

You've been very false to me
Now, for sometime past
When deceit comes in between
Friendship cannot last.

Love and friendship cannot live
Founded on a lie
Therefore, that we part to day
Who's to blame? Not I."

UNTITLED

I cannot go to the skies, their spanning arches
Spring too high to be scaled by human marches;
But the skies bend down with myriad stars and holy,
Sometimes bend to the soul of me the lowly.

Oh dear God, Creator of beauty, Sender
Of light, of air, of worlds of infinite splendor,
Grant to me the miracle past believing,
Breadth and cleaness of soul for such receiving.

Angels of power to obey Jehovah's orders
Sweep the dust from my heart and enlarge its borders,
Widen the space beclogged by the world's depression,
Make it meet for the glory of sky possession.

Who hath trouble of tears or life's repining
When in the soul the brilliant stars are shining?
Prizes of earth are mean, its pleasures grimmer
And the pitiful woes of time grow dim and dimmer.
I shall sleep when the gaudy day is over,
Sweetly sleep beneath my flower strewn cover.
I cannot go to the skies with my feet unsteady,
But the skies bend down and fill my soul already.
(Belmar, NJ)

UNTITLED

I met a little happiness coming my way
A shy little happiness coming my way
I held out my hand, "Don't you think you can stay
Pretty little happiness coming my way?"

I coaxed and I coaxed, and I said with a sigh
"Nobody likes you half as much as I.
Welcome as a sunbeam in a blue sky
Stop—little happiness—Do not pass me by!"

She blinked and she blinked and said it's hardly true
That you need me as much as other folks do
Very well without me you seem to get along
With a lilt, and a grief, and a laugh and a song.

I looked little happiness squarely in the eye
"Maybe that's the truth—maybe it's a lie!
But go little happiness—I will let you pass
Leave me as you find me, calm, but rather dull—alas!
(July 1915)

AN INVITATION
For the INTELLIGENCER
"A little nonsense now and then,
Is relished by the best of men."

Inscribed particularly to "Pansy."
Will you come to my nice little hut by the sea?
The fishes are waiting for you and for me.
The porpoise is leaping, the codfish and whales
In anticipant welcome are wagging their tails.

Already the crabs in the weeds of Shark river,
Begin with coquettish excitement to quiver;
They stretch all their legs, to be ready to dart,
When through the clear water the hunting boats start.

Why, even the clams when at evening the tide
Sends them up on the shore with their shells open
wide,
Unite with the oysters in wishing to be
Cooked up in a pate for you and for me.

Then come to my cottage, dear woman, dear man!
Carpe diem! Leave sadness at home—if you can.
Time enough, time enough when you go back again,
To take up life's burden, to suffer life's pain.

Forget for the moment, and try to be gay,
Pack your cares and your troubles securely away,
With your very fine clothes in a strong cedar box,
And fasten them in with the tightest of locks.
Bring an old flannel dress and an old pair of shoon;
And a soul that with nature is finely attune;
Above all—don't forget—my dear friends, as you
start

To bring a sweet temper, and bring a good heart.
We will sit on the shore all the bright sunny day.
We will watch the soft skies; we will watch the waves
play;
We will fancy we're mermaids; and as we recline
Why—I can comb your hair and you can comb mine.

Or at night, by the light of the moon and the star,
We will float in a boat; I will take my guitar,
We will ride o'er the spot where the treasure is hid,
The silver and gold of the dark Captain Kidd.

May the incoming tide bring us health and repose!
May the ebb of the tide carry off all our woes!
May the winds of the sea blow us strength; and the
rolls
Of the waves wash the weariness out of our souls!
(Ocean Beach.)

FOURTH OF JULY IN VENICE
SUNG AT CONSULATE DINNER

On the shores of the famed Adriatic
Surrounded by wave and by foam,
We pause on our footstep erratic
To think to day fondly of home.
To the deep beating heart of our nation
Our pulse thrills responsively too,
As we give with a keen jubilation
Three cheers for the red, white, and blue.

Let us cheer till our voices awaken
The slumbering Queen of the sea,
And San Marco's old lion, mistaken,
Will dream that Italia is free.
You artist, and you dilettante,
Whose heart throbs are loyal and true
Lift your glasses of Asti Spumante,
And drink to the red, white, and blue.

May we good Americans ever,
Whatever our object or aims,
Love our country and make an endeavor
To answer her indirect claims.
Our country may nothing distress her;
To her may we always be true,
The Republic forever—God bless her
And cherish her red, white, and blue.

WHEN BRIDGET SWEEPS THE ROOM

When Bridget sweeps the room
She waves an angry broom,
Upon the floor she wages war
    When Bridget sweeps the room.

She comes like a gust
And raises the dust,
She pounds the floors
And bangs the doors,
The spiders fly ·
And so do I,
    When Bridget sweeps the room.

When I get up next day
My slippers are hidden away
In every case in a different place,
    When Bridget sweeps the room

The pictures are all
Awry on the wall,
There isn't a match
That's fit to scratch,
And in vain I grope
For my favorite soap,
    When Bridget sweeps the room.

TO MEMORY

To thee capricious memory, I commit
The sweet and beautiful moment of today!
And charge thee well to guard and cherish it
And wreathe it round with evergreen and bay,
That it may live forever through the strife,
The jangle, and vicissitudes of life.
Thou, who hast faithful kept and keepest yet
So many things t'were better to forget;
Thou, who doest dog forever in my track
Storing the sad and bitter in thy pack;
Failing to grasp of happiness thy share;
Hoarding the foolish with such jealous care;
Dost thou not feel regret at thine own folly
To cherish thus but grief and melancholy?
Dost never wish a conserve for contrasting
With thine accustomed? Make this moment lasting
Put this within thy jar to flavor it
And it may make thee brighten up a bit.

Then shall I find thy company more pleasant
And sweeter to me than it is at present.

"FEAR GOD"

"Fear God."
Indeed, Theology, you make me laugh
With strange ideas. Do the smothering, half
Asphyxiated fear fresh air? Does he
Dying of thirst, fresh water fear to see
O Irony! Who can Fear God?

Fear man?
Yes. With his blundering, pathetic brain,
His cruel arrogance, strutting disdain
His limitations, self-complacencies; an ant
Ambitious to scale heaven, adamant
In vengeance. O Priest!
Fear Man.

Fear beast;
Savage, bloodthirsty, quadruped or human,
Fear lions, tigers, foxes, babe or woman,
Retail or wholesale robber, vampire, he
Who sucks his brother's blood; scab of humanity
Fear pride and greed of pelf;
Fear beast.

Fear thyself;
The enemy within thy gates. Perhaps
Most dangerous of all his subtle traps;
That hydra-headed self, which thou dost slay,
Resurgent springs to life again each day
To tempt thee yet to fall;
Fear self.

Fear all;
The social fabric, built about us; Law,

Mis-shaped abortion—ape, arousing awe
In lion skin of Justice. Tremble at
Lies, low ideas, false interpretations that
Wrest Scripture unto evil;
Fear all.

Fear the Devil;
That great spirit of hate, that baleful will;
The antipodal of Good—that would work ill;
The black breeder of bad—poison of joys,
Sibilant serpent of sin that ever destroys,
Chafing to use his rod.
Fear the Devil.

"Fear God"?
Ask easier task. Ask that of Sisyphus;
This is too hard that you demand of us.
Blind, to fear light—heart-frosted to fear heat?
Sin, to fear absolution, love complete?
Hearts to fear good and bright?
Or hungry souls, delight?

"Fear God"?
Fear all thing's else in sky, or earth, or sea!
O Jesu! Nazarene! slain on Calvary!
God, God! when everything is said and done,
Thou art the joy and hope of every one!
And, blest in thee,
Each sobbing soul seeks rest in thee.

"Fear God"?
If I were lying deep in Hell, unshriven,
Satan triumphant, sins all unforgiven,
Bound down—at voice of God my soul

would break
Its shackles, and through fire and brimstone make
Way to its magnet—God!

Deus, recipe nos omnes! Amen.
(Belmar, NJ)

FOR BRADLEY—OUR BRADLEY

At Monmouth Junction, long ago,
Your Grandsires stood against the foe;
But you have a war that's more dangerous far,
So rally for Senator Bradley.

    CHORUS
For Bradley,—James Bradley
The people are needing you sadly!
Hurrah for the Knight who is ready to fight;
We'll make him a Senator gladly.
For Bradley, James Bradley,
Is spirited, honest and bright!

The forces of evil are serried and strong,
The moment is coming to smite the wrong.
It needs a firm hand to deliver the land;
"And what is the matter" with Bradley?

    CHORUS
For Bradley, James Bradley,
The people are needing you sadly.
It needs a firm hand to deliver the land;
So rally for Senator Bradley,
For Bradley, Beach Bradley
Has plenty of courage and "sand!"
Not all honest men of New Jersey, do
Just vote as your conscience spurs ye to;
Come out of your fogs and your cranberry bogs
And rally for Senator Bradley.—CHORUS

Put party and prejudice bravely aside,
Come forward and banish political pride.
And will you be led by the Jockies instead

Of a practical thinker, like Bradley—CHORUS.

Down with the insolent flaunting of sin,
Help to make law and sobriety win.
To wipe out the stain of the State and regain
It's glory—rely upon Bradley.—CHORUS.

Three cheers for the hero of Asbury Park!
Three for the man who is up to the mark!
Hurrah for his grit, for his pluck and his wit,
And make him a Senator gladly.
    CHORUS.

Oh Bradley, Our Bradley,
The Devil is battling you madly!
"You do such things, and you say such things"
That you're rattling the evil one badly.
Oh Bradley, Our Bradley,
The Devil is pensive and sad.
(Belmar, NJ)

THE BELL OF LANCASTER

Fair are the fields of Lancaster,
And rich in corn and grain;
Brightly the sun at Lancaster
Shines over hill and plain;
There in the spring the garden beds
With yellow flowers bloom gay;
The butterflies and honey bees
Surround them all the day.
    Oh, bell—sad bell,
    Cease thy knell!

And I would go to Lancaster,
And I would happy be!
There are kind hearts at Lancaster,
And hands held out to me;
And voices that I know and love
Salute me as I pass;
But voices I still better knew
I hear no more—alas!
    Oh, bell—sad bell,
    Cease thy knell!

On a hill-slope at Lancaster,
With fair, outlying view,
Shadowed by fleecy clouds that pass,
Above in ether blue;
There—underneath the grassy sod,
With dandelions bespread,
Waiting the resurrection—lie
The ashes of my dead.
    Oh, bell—sad bell,
    Cease thy knell!

Oh, birds, sweet birds of Lancaster,
Sing out your loudest strain!
Try if you may not drown the sound
That fills my heart with pain!
For, evermore at Lancaster,
Pulsating in the air,
I hear the tolling of a bell
That calleth not to prayer.
 Oh, bell—sad bell,
  Cease thy knell!

Oh, tolling bell of Lancaster,
Whatever I may do—
However strive to close my ears,
You vibrate through and through.
Whatever song I listen to
Your cadence throbs apart;
Mid laugh and jest I feel your stroke
Beat heavy on my heart.
 Oh, bell—sad bell,
  Cease thy knell!

Oh, cruel bell of Lancaster!
Bronze hath not ruth of pain,
Else surely thou wouldst pity take
And cease thy minor strain.
Oh, shining sun of Lancaster,
For me you shine no more!
Oh, singing birds of Lancaster,
Ye cannot heal my sore!
 Oh, bell—cruel bell,
  Thou wilt never cease to knell!

ASHES AND CINDER

Ho! Rich men at your festal board,
What pleasure take ye in your hoard?
Earth's rarest gifts it will not buy,
And that ye know as well as I.

Eternal truth will still prevail.
Tho nations rise and races fail,
From Dresden plate or Sevres cup
Inexorable law ye sup.

And tho your keys be strong and stout.
They cannot lock earth's mockery out.
Whatever costly wine ye sip
Is blent with ashes on your lip.

Ye cannot buy the gifts most rare.
Health, beauty, or relief from care;
Leisure, good heart, ye cannot buy,
And that ye know as well as I.

Go, build ye high, if you would keep
Your memory lasting when you sleep.
Such tombs as the Scaligeri did,
Or pyramids where Pharaohs hid.

Well,—Pharaoh, dragged from rifled halls,
Now decks th' Egyptian museum walls.
His gold and power could purchase not
Exemption from the common lot.

Say, tell me do you really prize
The envy of the vulgar eyes?
When the heart hungers for the true,

Does mob laudation comfort you?

Can the best dress you walk within
Improve the texture of your skin?

Or triumph's crowning laurel wreath
Alter the skull it binds beneath?

Owners of gold, not lacking wit,
Ye know the impotence of it.
Your dearest wish ye cannot buy.
And that ye know—better than I
(Washington, DC)

DAWN

Dawn came into the drowsy world,
The curtains of night she softly furled.

She sang to the world austere and gray,
"Get ready—get ready to meet the day."

She put the sleepy stars to bed,
And tinted the fleecy clouds with red;

She gilded the tops of the tallest trees,
And freed the freshest morning breeze.

Evil shades and the sins of night
Fled away from her honest sight.

The sick man turned his weary eyes
To greet her coming in the skies.

"Would God," she cried, to souls in grief,
"I would to God I could bring relief."

She roused the farmer's wife, "Get up,
Prepare the platter, prepare the cup"

"Out in the barn the cows are lowing,
And clover heads await their mowing."

She roused the birds to life and song,
And opened buds as she passed along.

Oh! the smell of the woods was sweet,
When wild flowers bloomed beneath her feet
But when she saw the Lord of Day,

Modest Dawn slipped out of the way.
(Belmar, NJ)

The wooded hills of Francisvale*
Sound to-night with Sultan's wail,
Sultan, big dog and loyal-hearted
From his dear mistress has been parted.

And—bitter drop within the cup—
Mine was the voice that gave him up;
Mine was the hand that led him there.
And left him frantic with despair.

Justice demanded sacrifice;
On his black head was set a price;
For chicken rights must be protected
And neighboring farms must be respected.

Dog howls aloud to heaven his woes;
But woman, silent, onward goes,
With one more added to her share
Of griefs humanity must bear.

Renunciation is our laws,
Good-bye, rough head and shaggy paw.

Sultan, whose love surpassed the human,
Surpassed the love of man to woman.

He never criticised; his trust
Was noble, absolute and just.
In woe or weal, in sun or shine,

---

* Home for dogs in Radnor, PA

For good or ill, his heart was mine.
Little recked he what gown was worn,
Fashioned and gay, plain or forlorn;
Wrinkled or smooth, bright or distrest,
Mine was the face he loved the best.

He never claimed I must obey;
He never took my vote away;
He never said I had no soul,
Nor bartered troth for stern control.

O'er obstacle or chasm wide,
With mighty bound he sought my side,
And his black head would tightly press
Against me, claiming my caress.

And not the wisest or the wittiest
Could lure him from me, nor the prettiest.

Scant wonder then, since we must part,
Tears swell from my tumultuos heart.

At Windsor Forges chickens now
Triumphant perch on bush and bough;
And jubilant, with shrilly crow,
Rejoice o'er their departed foe.

They have their right, but I shall hate
All summer this decree of fate
Cackle and strut are hard to see,
Sultan, when I remember thee.

("The following poem was written for the late grand Centennial Tea Party in Philadelphia, by Miss Blanche Nevin, the accomplished daughter of President Nevin. It was originally published in the *Press*, but we know our readers, among whom Miss N. is so well known, will thank us for re-publishing it with the several corrections which errors in its former publication call for.")

OUR TEA PARTY

Lift up, lift up your steamy cup
And drink a toast with me;
"Our hard-bought land and noble band,
Who fought to set her free!"
Let no rude alcoholic fire,
Inspire a toast so grand,
Not brandy's shine, nor the red wine,
Make steady heart and hand
We want to-night some liquor bright,
On which all tastes agree:
So, "Polly, put the kettle on,
We'll all take tea!"

Historic cup! Drink, drink it up,
As mermaids down below
Gulped it one day in Boston Bay,
A hundred years ago;
Historic cup! Let grave and gay,
Young, old, and man and woman,
Quaff tea to-night with equal right—
The right of being human.
Here is no lack of green and black,
Of Oolong and Bohea;
So, "Polly, put the kettle on,
We'll all take tea!"

Our glorious toast: the land we boast—
God keep her gloriously!
Free from the strain of foreign rein,
From home oppression free—
Free from the prejudice of caste,
From persecuting sect—
Free from all lies, free to be wise,
As conscience shall direct;
To see the true, the right to do,
For this may we be free—
Free from all shame on our good name,
Free—from the tax on tea.

Yes, Polly, put the kettle on,
And as its steams arise,
We'll read like Watt, from the tea-pot,
A lesson to the wise.
This little puff about our tea,
It was that cleared the track
For Freedom's march, for Victory's auch,
And scalded tyrants back!
We're free to-day from foreign sway;
That such we still may be,
Dear Polly, keep your kettle hot,
We'll all take tea!

MRS. BAUMGARDNER'S GIVING A PARTY

Tira-la-la! Tira-lo-lo
"Over the Hills and away we go,"
To the spot where waffles are brown, we know
And the chickens broil in the gra-a-avy.

Motorman, motorman, tearing away,
Take us all up on your trolley;
Take us away for a spin to-day,
The ladies are out to be jolly.

Tira-la-la! Tira-lo-lo!
Off on the trolley, I told you so,
To the spot where the waffles are brown, you know
And the chickens broil in the gra-a-avy.

Cribbage a moment from worry and care,
Give it to innocent folly;
Maybe you'll find as we're taking the air,
Trouble blows off of the trolley.
Tira-la! Tira la! Lo-lo-lo!
Fresh on the trolley the winds do blow,
As to our supper away we go,
Where the chickens broil in the gra-a-avy.

Happy to-day,
Merry and gay,
Laugh while we may;
Spinning away,
"Nothing to pay,"
Didn't I say—

Mrs. Baumgardner's giving a party!
(Lancaster, August 30, 1894)

THE SNAKE AND THE BEE
After Metastasio

Snake and Bee go browsing over
Hill and valley, grass and clover

Eager each upon his quest
Choosing that he loveth best

While within the Bee the food
Turns to honey, sweet and good;

In the Serpent it will change
Into poison, bad and strange.

Jesus, let the eyes that read
Note the moral and give heed.

Life, which close environs thee,
Holds each possibility.

May our days then, fellow-man
Bring forth honey if we can.
(New York City)

THE RE-INCARNATION OF ELAINE AND LANCELOT

Dedicated to the Second Regiment, New Jersey
Volunteers.
"Nous avons change tout cela"
(Elaine loquitur.)

"Ah wo is me, my Lancelot,
That soon thy form must vanish,
Since thou across the southern sea
Must go fight the Spanish.

Accursed the parlous Congressmen
Who rushed the battle on!
Accursed the bush they hide behind
Until the war is done!

"And shall I weave a silken sleeve
With broiderie fine and gay;
My colors bright, most noble knight,
To deck thee in the fray?

"Full fain am I my lily hand
To prick for thy dear sake.
But tell me what my Lancelot
Prefers that I should make?"

"You're very kind," quod Lancelot,
"And since I understand
It's useful in the Cuban clime
I'd like a flannel band."

Then swiftly, swiftly she fled up
Unto her bower high,
Of flannel fine she cut a band—

She stopped not to sigh.
(Elaine sings.)

"Girdle him round, good flannel band,
Girdle the soldier round;
Sailing on ocean or marching on land
Sleeping on poisonous ground,
Wounded and sore in the desperate strife,
Fever and famine assailing his life,
Help to preserve him to mother and wife,
Oh, girdle the soldier round, around—
Girdle him round!

"Girdle him round, good homely band,
Girdle the soldier round.
Tenderest care for the men of our land
Into thy tapes is bound.
Aid thou the prayers of the women to save
Lives that are precious and patient and brave
From hospital horror or widening grave,
Oh, girdle the soldier round, around—
Girdle him round!

"Girdle him round, good flannel band,
Girdle the soldier round.
In the damp morass and malarious grass,
Where the spider and snake abound.
I would that my fingers with mystical charms
Might render thee potent to ward away harms,
And bring him again where my heart and my arms
Might girdle the soldier round, around—
Girdle him round!"
She stitched and sang and sang and stitched,
And pricked her lily hand;

Eftsoon brought back to Lancelot
A wholesome flannel band.

"It seemeth good " quod Lancelot,
And looked it calmly o'er,
The while Elaine, with spirit meed,
Cried, "What can I do more?"

"What more, what more, my Lancelot
Can needle do for thee?"

Again she raised the plaintive note
With threat of broiderie.

"You're very kind," quod Lancelot,
American was he,
"A housewife, since you mention it,
Would very handy be."

And she has ta'en the trolley-car
And ridden to the Park,
And there, intrenched behind his bar,
She found the dry-goods clerk.

"Oh, gie me of the covert cloth,
I want it fine and blue,
Whereof I may a housewife make
To give my lover true."

He stared at her, he glared at her
And haughty was his mien;
"We haven't got no covert cloth,
But here's pink bombazine."
Incontinent she turned and fled

Adown the crowded aisle,
While nasal voice pursuant said,
"Blue covert's not the style."
But hunting here and hunting there
She sought and sought and sought,
Until she found blue covert cloth,
Whereof she lavish bought.

Once more within her bower high
She tore the stuff in rolls,
And strongly bound a housewife round
And worked five buttonholes;

And in each little pocket put
Of thread an ample store,
Needles and buttons, safety-pins
A dozen, less or more.

A tiny comb, a scissors blunt,
Shoelaces made of leather,
A thinble, and some plasters used
To stick small wounds together.

(Sings)
"O little housewife,
Go, little housewife;
Be a little housewife good, good, good.
Be a steady housewife,
Be a steady housewife,
As every little housewife should, should, should.

"O little housewife,
Sew, little housewife;
Be a little housewife true, true, true,
Mend him, little housewife,
Tend him, little housewife,

As loving little housewives do, do, do."

Then once again to Lancelot
She hied with footstep fleet,
And laid the finished housewife down
In triumph at his feet.

Never a word quod Lancelot,
But gazed a little while,
And turned that housewife in and out,
And gave a grimlie smile.

"Speak out, speak out, my Lancelot;
What woman's wit can do
Or brain devise, that will I try
To aid and comfort you."

"You're very kind," quod Lancelot,
"And since you thus incline
To help, it's my opinion that
Pajamas would be fine!"

"Now will I take my bicycle
And spin the country over,
And trust me will not fail to find
Pajamas for my lover."

(Sings.)
"Wheel on, wheel on, my bicycle,
Away from musty sorrow;
Let nature's breezes bring me strength
And freshness for tomorrow.
"Wheel on, wheel on, O bicycle!
May each of thy gyrations

Carry us into broader life,
Widen our limitations.

"Wheel on, wheel on, O bicycle,
Fulfil thy bouyant mission;
Untwist thy wheels of progress from
The cobwebs of tradition.

"Wheel off, wheel off, O bicycle,
From narrow life and meanness,
And bring us to the flowery fields
Of health and joy and cleanness."

Thus singing on her bicycle
She spun the country over;
Of proper kind, she could not find
Pajamas for her lover.

Then took she silk of India
And cut them out and made them,
And ceased not to sing and stitch
Till at his feet she laid them.

"A boon, a boon, O Lancelot,
I crave a boon of thee!"
"Damsel, say on," replied that knight,
"What do you wish of me?"

"To seek thee when the battle's o'er,
To bear thee from the field,
To give thee care and medicine
Until thy wounds be healed;
"To nurse thee well, to cool thy brow
Should maddening fever fret thee."

"It may not be," quod Lancelot, "now,
For Sternberg will not let thee."

"Alack, alack!" cried out Elaine
"Full hapless is my fate,
To be bereft of usefulness,
Why was I born so late?

"For who before the present war
Hath questioned women's right
To follow where their bleeding mates
Lie wounded in the fight;

"To watch them in their hours of pain
When feverish pulses rise;
To nurse them back to health again
Or close their dying eyes?

"The savage and the civilized,
The publican and priest,
Each jealous partisan of sex
Hath left us this at least.

"And must this scanty heritage
Be wrested by the great
Republican America
In 1898?
"Our voice in government is hushed,
Our judgment scorned and banished;
From all romance of history
And art our form has vanished.

"No more as goddess or as saint,
In hierarchy we're placed,

From civic ceremony we
Are utterly effaced.

"Forsooth—oh, great Male-ocracy
Your greed is hardly nice,
To grudge our last undoubted right
Of patient sacrifice!

"To fold our eager, helpful hands
From nursing you debarred;
In very truth, my Lancelot,
It seems a little hard."

Armed cap-a-pie marched Lancelot
Off to the Cuban land,
Pajamas and his housewife packed,
He wore his flannel band.

Americanus homo, he
Neglecting for his clubs
Americanam feminam
Acclimated to snubs.

She watched awhile his hurrying read,
Then turned to help her mother,
"Sister, your nose and eyes look red!"
Remarked her little brother.
Scant time had she throughout the day
For moping over woes;
She dusted all the bric-a-brac
And darned the family hose.

She heard another brother read,
To practise his oration

Composed for graduating day
On female education;

Went to the parlor, to receive
The Rev. Slimkin's call
(He talked of marriage—favoring
The opinions of St. Paul);

Wrote to condole with Cousin Sue,
Congratulated Lizzie,
Made "Papa dear" a new cravat,
And all the day was busy.

But when at night she lay in bed
And looked out at the stars,
And meditated dreamily
Of men and puzzling wars,

She thought, "If I could pine and die,
And down the river float,
Draped all in silken cramoisie,
Laid out upon a boat,

With folded hands and hair unbound,
And lilies covering me,
Steered by an old dumb servitor,
How lovely that would be!

"And if he read a bit of note
A dead girl brought so sadly,
Why then—perhaps—that Lancelot
Would feel a little badly."

Into her window gazed the stars,

The old stars calm and deep;
And murmuring, "No such luck for me,"
Elaine fell fast asleep.
(Belmar, NJ)

REGINA HATH ASKED ME TO WRITE

Regina hath asked me to write!
Oh, what would I give to be bright?
Here's a chance to encircle my name
With a halo of posthumous fame.
The crucial moment has come
And behold I am stupid and dumb.

Oh! What can a poor woman do
Or say that would interest you?
And if I dared venture to try
You would know it all better than I.
"There is nothing new under the sun?
Was said ere our race was begun.
All knowledge, all wisdom, all wit
By somebody else has been writ
So I find when my pen I up-take
I have no observations to make

Be content then Regina, dear dame
If I simply bequeathe you my name
        Which is
            BLANCHE

THE BANYAN TREE

That Banyan tree disturbeth me
I do not like that Banyan tree

Ambitious in its every act,
It hath not reason grace nor tact
The queerest thing I ever did see
It really is the Banyan tree.
Its roots are thick, are thin, are flat,
Are twisted this way, spindled that.
It hath not logic, sense nor rule
And generally plays the fool.
That greedy tree it wants the earth
Is ever in continuous birth.

Surely 'twere better and more wise
Consistently to seek the skies
To follow some especial bent
Some law in its development.
But no obedient to each whim,
To each caprice which seizes him,
That Banyan tree without a plan
Behaves exactly like—a *man*

Elaborate in, elaborate out,
It tines and twists itself about
Burst with pretention to be wise
Turns back to earth from half won skies
Uplifts towards heaven returns to dust,
And isn't at all a thing to trust.
That Banyan tree, that Banyan tree
It is not what it ought to be.

It hath not reason law nor rule,
And generally plays the fool.

(Palm Beach, FL)

HERE'S TO PETER BARR

I traveled long and traveled far
And in Japan met Peter Barr.

Oh, Lady touch your light guitar
And sing Scotch songs, cried Peter Barr

Sing Annie Laurie, Lochinvar
And Bonnie Doon, said Peter Barr.

Each blue eye twinkled like a star
Beneath the brows of Peter Barr.

He's learned, a list of letters are
Tacked to the name of Peter Barr.

In science few are on a par
And none excel wise Peter Barr

His conquests are of peace, not war
A botanist is Peter Barr.

Wielding no sword or scimitar
Thinker and worker, Peter Barr.

Disarmament and Russian Czar
Would suit precisely Peter Barr.

Yet like the violent Sirdar
Tombs might be robbed by Peter Barr.

No quarrel yet has chanced to mar
My harmony with Peter Barr

Though we discuss we never spar
I'm calm, and so is Peter Barr.

But when I left it seemed to jar
That singing club of Peter Barr.

"Next Sunday I will take a car
And come down too" said Peter Barr

Gallant as Henry of Navarre
Though unbeplumed, is Peter Barr!

Thy faithful soul would stick like tar
In love or friendship Peter Barr.

Forever green as cinnobar
Shall be thy memory Peter Barr.

Today I toast thee from afar
Dear chatty Scotchman, Peter Barr.

Beside the steaming samovar
Here's to the health of Peter Barr!

(Kamakura, Japan, 1899)

KOON YAM GODDESS OF MERCY

When Koon Yam went to Hades, it is said,
She, whose heart was warm and kind,
Was much troubled in her mind,
Such harsh punishment to find
    Of the dead
        Wicked dead.

With sympathy her heart was like to break.
So, she fell upon her knees
And besought the Gods to please
Have compassion upon these
    For her sake
        Pity's sake.

Straightway sweet flowers fell 'round her
    from above
And as they touched the ground,
All the wicked ones unbound,
Within Paradise were found
    Through her love;
        Holy love.

Then frightened were the rulers down below.
"Oh, we cannot have such things
What perplexity she brings!"
Said the dark assembled kings,
    "She must go
        really go."

So they sent her back to Canton in a trice,
To the land of mortal men,

Reincarnate once again;

Where they built her temple then
   Is nice,
      Very nice!
(Canton, March 26, 1899)

NEW YEAR'S 1914

Out of my window, early today
I saw the New Year heading this way:
Over the ocean restless and grey
The ocean ruminant, panting and grey
   Ahoy! Ahoy!

Born of the sunlight, born of the sky
Sent to this world from the Power on high,
Bearing a benison. Hope draweth nigh,
Laugh now, ye sorrowful, Hope draweth nigh
   Ahoy! Ahoy!

Hither the New Year comes brilliant, and lo
Lights all the greyness, above and below,
Mounts the horizon a roseate glow
Tint all the mauves with the roseate glow,
   Ahoy! Ahoy!

Courage, downhearted, and fold away care,
While we have New Years we need not despair,
Life from the Infinite colors the air
Faith, Hope and Charity color the air.

(Written for the Altoona Tribune)

SEPARATION

It is not the mountain, it is not the land
It is not the deep wide sea
And the stretch of the desert sand
That can separate you and me
    Sweetheart,
Can separate you and me.

Hands may clasp and tighten and hold
And heart be pressed to heart
Yet only shadows the arms enfold
If souls have grown apart
    Sweetheart
If souls have grown apart.

Not the gallop of racing horse
Can carry us side from side
Not the steam or electric force
Can make the distance wide
    Sweetheart
Can make the distance wide.

But the cruel thought, the harsh distrust
The word that biteth sore
Each from each apart could thrust
So far we might meet no more
    Sweetheart
In this world nevermore.
(Lancaster, PA)

TO MISS HELEN OUTERBRIDGE

Oh! list to the song I invented this morning,
And do not be scorning
My fugitive verse:
For I had not the time, dear,
To polish my rhyme, dear;
Just try to be thankful it isn't much worse.

Oh! here's to Tom Moore, and here's also to Byron
(That masculine siren)
And peace to each soul
If waiting aweary
Outside with the Peri,
(I don't mean the Peary who found the North Pole).
And here's to Miranda, that tempest tossed Lady,
Who found these groves shady
A haven of rest.
And Ariel delightful
And Caliban spiteful,
When wrecked on the shores of this Island possest.

And here's to Mark Twain, since my muse has
her stilts on,
To President Wilson;
To me and to you
To glad folks and sad folks,
A blessing to all—and to Chittenden too.

I cannot write more for my pen is too rusty,
My thoughts are too musty
Your grace I implore
But give a cheer hearty
To Miss Helen's party
To her, to Bermuda—and then to Tom Moore.

ALL SAINTS' DAY
(Il Journo des Morti)

I sit by the firelight alone
'Mid shadows, for daylight has fled;
There is none to be grieved at my moan,
And this is the day of the Dead,

The light has gone out of the sky
The _____ ____ cold from the earth
I sit by my firelight, and cry
"Oh Lazarus, come forth!"

Oh, ye who profoundly do sleep
Through the pains and the joys of the year
In the graves where we buried you deep,
To-night rise and live with me here!
Once again claim your desolate place;
Once again, as around me ye come,
Let me gaze on each dear, pallid face;
Once again open lips that are dumb!

Speak! Speak that my soul may rejoice!
Let us talk as together of yore,
My ears greet the sound of each voice,
And listen each cadence once more.
Do ye dwell in a region of bliss,
Where sorrow and pain all forgot
Consoles you for parting from this?
Does memory haunt you or not?

Is death such a joyful relief?
Have ye never a pain or a tear?
Have ye never a sorrow or grief,
And never a shudder or fear?

Have ye looked on the face of our Lord,
And suddenly found you appeased,
Your health and your courage restored,
Your agony over and ceased?

Is the music of Heaven so sweet,
Are Christ and the angels so dear,
Is your rapture so full and complete,
That you have not a thought of us here?
And oh, as ye pulsate and throb
In Heaven's harmonious sphere,
Do ye never responsively sob
To the wail at your vanishing here?

Give answer, give answer, my Dead?
The night wanes apace, and the flashes
From embers no longer are red
As I cower low down to the ashes.
Your faces are drifting away,
I question you ever in vain;
No longer ye tarrying stay,
But fade from my vision again.

Still never a word do ye say,
Dissolving in ether afar.
Oh, speak ere ye vanish away!
How terribly silent ye are!
Yet linger one moment, my Dad,
And the hands whose each movement
I know
Place soft on my desolate head,
And bless me, and smile ere ye go.

But out of my window the dawn

Of the day is beginning—and hark!
Full throated and clear on the lawn,
The earliest note of the lark!
And in the mysterious east
Breaks dimly the light of to-morrow;
The darkness is over, and ceased
My vigil of love and of sorrow.

No longer the day of the dead,
For the day of the living is here;
Arise to the dawn that is red,
Arise to the dawn that is clear!
And courage, my heart, without grieving!
Once more lay thy dead 'neath the sod;
Go forth to the world that is living,
And trust in the mercy of God.

(Washington, DC)

Seven

Anecdotal Elaboration Of Blanche's Life

Mary Bell Stahr wrote in1882:

One summer, Blanche wished to paint a portrait of my father, Dr. John Stahr, President of F & M College (1890-1909).

He was to put on his doctor's gown and go up to the college and stand by the brass Eagle lectern, which was a memorial gift of the Nevin family to the College.

Poor father! He would stand for hours on a hot day and would get tired. Miss Blanche got tired too! The portrait was ghastly and she never finished it.[25,Vol. 1]*

Miss Blanche was a very affectionate woman and was fond of father and mother. She was a delightful person, with lots of fun in her. Miss Alice Nevin was more dignified and sober."[25]

---

* It is not unusual for the subject to not like their portrait.

LION DEDICATION CEREMONY

Lancaster newspapers devoted a column and a half to the dedication ceremony as the city received Blanche's gift of the lion fountain on June 17, 1905.

The master of ceremonies and first speaker was Francis Bowes Sayres, youngest of Blanche's nephews. Rev. Dr. J. C. Bowman of Reformed Theological Seminary made the invocation. The blessing of the water for the dedication by the Rev. Anthony Kaul, rector of St. Anthony's Catholic Church was very unique. Addresses were made by Dr. William Hayes Ward, Editor of *NY Independent*, who spoke on the subject of "Civic Beauty," Rev. Dr. J. M. Schick, pastor of the German Reformed Church of Washington, DC, who took the subject "The Life and Work of Dr. Nevin," Rev. Dr. J. S. Stahr, and Dr. W. F. Faber of Lockport, NY, who also spoke of Dr. Nevin and his life as a friend and colleague.

Miss Nevin pulled the cord that released the American flag covering the majestic lion, formally presenting the sculpture fountain to Mayor Cummings on behalf of the city of Lancaster. Te Deum and Auld Lang Syne were sung by the crowd of thousands, accompanied by the Iroquois Band. To complete the program, Blanche was presented with a magnificent bouquet of American Beauty roses from the City Councilman.

The guests in attendance and the speakers at the dedicatory exercises were entertained at breakfast by Miss Alice Nevin and Mrs. Robert H. Sayre, of Bethlehem, at Miss Alice's home on Lancaster Avenue.

RESTORATION OF WINDSOR FORGE
BY ROBERT SIMPSON, *THE RAMBLER*, WHO WORKED
FOR BLANCHE IN HIS YOUTH

Windsor Forge has always been owned by family members since David Jenkins bought it from Lardner, who was a member of the Provincial Council of Pennsylvania and a Philadelphia lawyer. John Jenkins, patentee, sold it to Branson, father of three daughters, and then his son-in-law Lardner became owner with his father-in-law Branson of the whole five forges and property.

Blanche purchased Windsor Hall from her cousin, Mrs. Catherine Reigart Cummins in 1897 for $18,000. (Blanche said 1899 in her Souvenir history for Berks County Historical Society.)

Mr. and Mrs. Cummins had lived in retirement for a number of years, but decided to return to New York City, where he had practiced law in the early 1890s. The mansion became neglected with no caretaker and renters.

Miss Nevin, who lived there for two years when she was 12 years old, seeing its condition, decided to buy it and renew it to a semblance of its former beauty, from a sense of family pride and to preserve it for posterity. The roof was poor, many panes of glass were broken, and the lawns, terraces and orchard were overgrown and over-run with cattle.

The late William J. McCaa had charge of the renovating and carpenters, painters, mechanics, and laborers in the summer of 1899, and from plans by Miss Nevin, soon changed the place to a habitable mansion once again. Miss Nevin then made it her home until her death, with the exception of the winter months.

She was a great traveler, visiting all parts of the world, and was a true cosmopolitan, knowing thoroughly the old countries from Oporto to Tokyo. She was a rare linguist, which greatly aided her travels. The wanderlust was no doubt acquired when she went abroad to study sculpture and painting. She had the means to satisfy her desire for foreign tutelage. She was dauntless and unafraid to pursue her studies among the bizarre Bohemian life of many artists' studios.[12]

To her friends and neighbors at Windsor Forge she seemed distant, odd, not easily approached. But the writer knows she always was courteous, kind at heart, and never intentionally ignored anyone. Often as she rode by driving "Bob," her first horse, she would scarcely notice the passersby, not because she thought herself above them, but simply because she was a visionary. Her thoughts were far away, seeking some inspiration of love, ardor, law, charity, or civilization to be expressed in some beautiful form by pen or scalpel.

To those who had access to her intimate social life she was a charming woman and was especially admired for unusual versatility. "It is not what you do. It is the way you do it that counts." She has been signally honored and few of us who have been her neighbors are aware to what extent she has been honored.[12]

BLANCHE'S GARDENS

With all the flower beds and vine arbor, Blanche also maintained a vegetable garden as everyone in the country did. There has not been a garden plan found, but perhaps she used the five-seed plan when dropping corn, if it was handed down to her.

One for the blackbird
One for the crow
One for the cutworm
And two to grow.

This plan was found in *The Messenger*, a church newspaper. The Nevins contributed articles—Alice and Patty (Martha), when they traveled abroad. There were poems, unsigned, that sound like Blanche's work. *The Messenger* was in the Evangelical Reformed Historical Society archives.

Blanche did have articles and poetry published in some magazines. She used the pseudonym of "Bianca" when she signed her writings, according to Rev. Amos Seldomridge.

Amos and Rev. John Weiler have been a great help. They both have been gathering Nevin and Sayre lore, with a special interest in Blanche's life.

THE FIRST JOHN JENKINS IN THE
CAERNARVON AREA

The first land grant of 400 acres was given to John Jenkins in his oldest son's, Jenkin Jenkins, name as *The Rambler* has written it. It was 1733. John Jenkins evidently had his own patent on land that he sold to Davies that was adjacent to the first property.

Nothing more seems to have been written about John and Jenkin Jenkins' work after selling the patent to Branson some nine years later.

In the book, *Pennsylvania: Colonial and Federal, a History,* a John Jenkins appears as being connected to the Susquehanna Company and the designating of proprietaries to some 40 persons, first coming. His group was charged with making a road to the Susquehanna River as well as measuring each person's land grant. Some of each proprietary was to have a designated space for a church, and school, and only upright persons were to be part of the receiving group of the land.

Somehow, John Jenkins seemed to escape being taken into custody by Sheriff Jennings when the others of his committee were caught.

So it seems the old stories of John hunting and fishing with Indians may have been in line with his business. The proprietaries had to dislodge the Indians first with agreements and wampum belts. He was rumored to be a surveyor, and that would fit this line of endeavor also.

John became involved in the Revolutionary War at some point, since his grave is one of the five Jenkins at Old Bangor Church marked with the 1776 (Revolutionary War) plaque.

It was John's son David who worked as bookkeeper for Branson and his son-in-law Lardner. And when Elizabeth Lardner died, he bought her shares and kept buying until he owned the five forges.

David bequested Windsor Forges and nearly three thousand acres of land to his eldest son Robert, and Robert was to pay brother William, builder of Wheatland, and his three sisters, Rebecca Wilson, Margaret Kreider, and Martha, unmarried, one thousand pounds each. It was 1798.

John Jenkins' mother-in-law Sara Aurelia Rush was said to be the first English girl child born in "Pennsy lands," or Pennsylvania.

LANCASTER COUNTY HISTORICAL SOCIETY ANNUAL OUTING TO OLD HISTORIC WINDSOR FORGE JULY 2, 1915

From the Lancaster County Historical Society minutes:

> Miss Blanche Nevin, the sculptress, entertains two hundred members and their friends, the forges, the associations (other societies) and addresses are as chronicled by the Stroller of *The New Era*.
>
> Members arrived from Lancaster by trolley to Blue Ball, where they were met by trucks, cushioned comfortably for passengers. Others came by automobile, and by afternoon more than a score of touring cars were parked about the premises.
>
> The receiving party was Miss Daisy Grubb, who will entertain the Historical Society at her home next year; Mrs. L. Heber Smith and Miss Mary G. Smith of Joanna Furnace in Chester County; Mr. and Mrs. William Potts of Valley Forge; Mrs. Rutter of Pine Forge; and Mrs. Brooks of Birdsboro. All are descendants of early ironmasters of Pennsylvania and assisted Miss Nevin to receive.[29]

Perhaps they distributed the souvenir glasses that Blanche had made for the occasion. They are said to have Windsor Forges* written on them and the year, 1915.

"Guests included clergymen, lawyers, artists, scholars, educators, scientists, authors, poets, broadminded businessmen, and connoisseurs and patrons of literature and fine arts.

Some were grouped about a huge water wheel used for an old forge and mounted now on some sculpture work of Miss Nevin.**

Three speakers, Henry W. Shoemaker, member of the American Legation at Berlin; Rev. George Israel Browne, dwelt on the bond between history and religion. Rev. Browne said, "that consciousness was the goal of evolution, and the highest consciousness included race as a whole, and so learned to value the past in the study of history. He was less than half a man who only had interest in the present."[25, Vol. 29]

The third orator of the day was young T. Roberts Appel. He was reported to be in fine fettle as he spoke at some length. He ended with "May no profane hand e'er mar these hallowed walls or desecrate this hallowed place. May time deal gently with you and all that you attract and shelter."[25, Vol. 29]

The picnic baskets brought by members provided variety in the food. The members explored the old 1742 buildings built to store food and ammunition.[25, Vol. 29] This is the one with an area enclosed with bars in the basement. No one seems to know for sure the purpose of the bars. To keep food safe or to keep people in isolation?

At the rear of the mansion is another fieldstone building that was used as a summer kitchen and wash house, and down the slope further there still remains the springhouse. These buildings are of sandstone, as is the early part of the mansion which is covered with stucco at the restoration by Blanche, it is thought. The old part was built about 1742 by Branson, partner of Lardner. Branson was Lardner's father-in-law and lived in it until David Jenkins bought the property. The old storage building may have been John Jenkins' home before he sold to Branson, after he had the grant of 400 acres for about nine years.

Names of some of the workers at the Windsor Forges were Silknetters, Eppihimers, Wilhours, Johnsons, Olds, and others.[25]

By 1875, the lower Windsor Forge was a mass of ruins. Blanche heard of the collapse of the last forge after she was living in Windsor after 1897 to sometime in the early 1900s.

At the time of the outing the large clay model of the lion on the front lawn was described as "looking like it would roar at your approach."[5]

The mansion and grounds were compared to Mt. Vernon, "the mansion massive, but thoroughly Colonial. The rooms spacious, halls wide, old fireplaces grand, carvings rare and beautiful."[5] No note made of the Italianate appearance of the exterior with the diamond-shaped small panes in the upper sash of each window.

The Jenkins, Olds, and Davies families were responsible for the birth of six forges at Windsor and Poole Forges.[5]

There is some erroneous belief here, since the Jenkins were never attached to Poole Forge. The connection was that Olds worked at Windsor Forge and learned the forge operation and then made the mill on the property he bought along the Conestoga from Edward Hughes into Poole Forge and operated it successfully until 1811.[57]

June 30, 1915, in a "Lancaster New Era" column describing the Lancaster Historical Society outing to Windsor Forges, Blanche had souvenirs for the guests. Dainty pattern glasses with the inscription, Windsor Forges, 1915; a picture of W. U. Hensel, and a photo of an iron gate designed by Parke E. Edwards.

Paintings in Blanche's home at this time were notable because of the three she imported, "Joseph Interpreting Pharaoh's Dream," "Joseph and Potiphor's Wife," and the third was thought to be St. Ann refusing the Crown of Thorns. Much of their significance was from their provenance of an early Doge's Palace. Blanche's own paintings were exhibited also. The author concludes, however, that Blanche preferred sculpture as her primary medium of expression.

A special dispatch to the *North American Newspaper* includes a picture of Blanche in a dark, short-sleeved, ruffled lace collar dress, standing behind the huge clay model for the lion, as if sculpting. It was placed squarely in front of the front entrance so that the approach to the front door afforded a good view. It was said the clay lion lasted several years before deterioration was so complete to cause its removal.

*Later information is that Poole Forge was said to have glasses as souvenirs. Perhaps they both had glasses for guests, or the story is another example of earlier poor memories.

*This may be the society secreatary's view of what the stone table was, but it is in error. It was never in mill or forge. Blanche had it cut to her specifications for table.

190

WOODROW WILSON, LOST AND FOUND

A signed bust of Woodrow Wilson, carved by Blanche in 1910, is located in Garland Hall on Homewood Campus of John Hopkins University of Baltimore, Maryland.

The original is in the US Capitol. The mold for the Wilson bust was spotted in an antique shop by Pendleton Herring, a staff member of Princeton at the time. He purchased it and returned it to Princeton. How the sculpture mold happened to be in an antique shop is not known. The Board of Trustees at Princeton authorized copies be made for every educational institution that Woodrow Wilson had been affiliated with, and so several were cut and distributed and that is why John Hopkins has a copy, as well as Princeton and the New Jersey Capitol in Trenton.

The clay model was formed at Sea Girt while the Wilsons and Blanche were vacationing in 1910. They had met on a cruise in 1907 or 1908 when vacationing in Bermuda. Wilson was in his last year at Princeton before being elected President of the United States.

Blanche dated the finished carving 1911, and it was the official Presidential bust during his term.

With the Wilson bust and the General Muhlenberg figure, Blanche has two sculptures in the nation's capitol.

Blanche's grandniece, Faith Sayre Schindler, had the family information necessary for this correct information of the whereabouts of the original Wilson.

YOUNG FRIEND FROM ITALY AND THE
LARGE LION SCULPTURE

At 85 years old, Robert E. Simpson recalled helping Miss Blanche Nevin prepare her lion statue for Reservoir Park in his youth.

Mr. Simpson's career spanned many years, as a teacher and co-director/owner of the Female Seminary at Marietta. He was *The Rambler* of the Caernarvon area with historic articles for the local gazette, *The Penny Saver,* and co-authored one of the annals on Conestoga Valley.

He was a young man of 35 when he worked for Blanche on the lion project. In his words:

Over 50 years ago, after the winter's sojourn in Europe, Miss Blanche Nevin brought home with her Angelo Pellichelli, a talented young Italian.

Angelo and I worked about Windsor Mansion's lawn and flower garden terrace many days that spring, trying to restore them to pristine beauty.

Miss Nevin had a driving horse by then that she named Champagne. One day in April, Angelo hitched Champagne to a neighbor's one-horse wagon and drove Miss Nevin to the brick kilns southeast of Honeybrook. There they secured a load of brick mud made to her specifications.

That afternoon Angelo and I placed the mud on a platform previously erected in front of the mansion. My next door neighbor, Skinny Hoffman, helped in making a platform of rocks, small stone, and cement. He wondered what in devil it was for.

We took great gobs of the mud and worked it with our hands until it was perfectly pliable and placed it in the position of a crude lion-shaped mass under the direction of Miss Nevin. We had to be careful to place it firmly and solidly, leaving no air bubbles especially in the bulky neck and head mass.

Next day Miss Nevin, with scalpel, began working on it. Often from my work I came and watched the adept hands of Miss Nevin at work. Gradually nose, mouth, eyes, and mane appeared and finally there was the perfect model of the lion.

Next came skilled artisans in metal statue work from the city who made a plaster cast of the lion. They made it in sections so it could be easily removed and reassembled to make the metal lion.

Finally the bronze lion was placed in Reservoir Park in Lancaster as you see it today.

The clay model in front of the mansion withstood the weather for many years before it deteriorated and was removed.

The next winter Angelo Pellichelli boarded with me to absorb some English, while Miss Nevin went to a warmer climate. The last I heard of Angelo he was teaching languages in a Chicago college."[12]

Rev. Amos Seldomridge tells the story of Dr. Stahr looking out a window at Franklin and Marshall College to see Blanche and several men near the front entrance to the campus. On inquiry it seems Blanche was preparing to install her lion memorial there. She was told without permission it couldn't be placed. How it became a landmark in Reservoir Park is probably another story.

THE BRASS EAGLE LECTERN

Writers have credited Blanche with creating the eagle lectern that was given to Franklin and Marshall as a memorial gift to honor Mrs. Martha Jenkins Nevin, wife of John W. Nevin. It was a gift from her five living children.

The brass eagle lectern was ordered by Rev. Robert Nevin from Thomas Potter and Sons, 361 Oxford Street., London West. It cost $400 and is said to be a replica of the celebrated Gothic Revival XIV century lectern in the Cathedral at Southwall or Southwell. It measures six feet, two inches to top of the standard and the spread wings of the eagle form the lectern space. At this writing in January 1996, it is in storage at Franklin and Marshall College.

It was on formal loan to the Old St. John's Church that stood at Mulberry and Orange Street by the old cemetery. The space where the church stood is a children's playground for the adjacent school. When St. John's closed to begin a new congregation, the lectern was returned to Franklin and Marshall College. Perhaps it will someday be on display in the Rothman Gallery or some protected space. In the ornamentation, the eagle is a symbol of the Resurrection.[60]

A NOTE ON OLD ST. JOHN'S

St. John's was a church that the President at Franklin and Marshall was instrumental in founding.

It was the church for German immigrants, and it's objective was to have a church home for "the Swiss immigrants that Stehlis Silk Mill was importing who were in danger of losing their souls..."[61]

The church was red brick with numerous stained glass windows and contained a mezzanine on three sides above the main church floor. Its membership died off and with suburbia expanding, the congregation merged with another and began a new church, the Church of the Apostles.

Reverend Amos Seldomridge was the last minister of St. John's.

The Eagle Lectern was loaned by F & M to Old St. John's for some time, but it was returned to F & M with the dismantling of the church.

THE LOAN SHOW

In 1912, the Loan Show was sponsored by the Iris Club and the Lancaster County Historical Society. It was held in the new Woolworth Building on the sixth and seventh floors.

On loan were 300 oil portraits, 125 miniatures, 50 or more watercolors, pastels, silhouettes, gold and silver medallions and medals, and bronze and marble busts.[25, Vol. 16]

Blanche served on the Auxiliary Committee, as did her sister Alice. Blanche also was on the special committee for busts and medals. Redmond Conyingham and Henry Chapman also served on that committee.

Blanche exhibited her bronze sculpture of Woodrow Wilson and the now lost bust of Catherine Carmichael Jenkins, her grandmother. The following is Blanche's resume in The Loan Show book.

"Blanche Nevin, daughter of John Williamson Nevin and sister of Robert Jenkins Nevin of Rome. Sister of Alice and Martha Finley Nevin Sayre.

Of Pennsylvania stock; studied at various places, chiefly Rome and The Royal Academy of Venice under Ferrari, and in her own studio in Carrara, Florence. Has traveled extensively in her own country and very widely abroad. Works spasmodically and interruptedly. Has produced statues and busts, among them the statue of Muhlenberg in the Capitol, Washington, DC. Has erected two memorial fountains at Lancaster, PA; paints portraits, sketches, and studies, and a writer of verses.

Some works were a portrait bust of Woodrow Wilson done from life at Sea Girt in the summer of 1910, small model of the sphinx and a restoration of the Naples torso of Victory.

Member of the Royal Arts of England; a Fellow of the Geographical Society of New York; Acorn Club of Philadelphia; and Historical Society of Lancaster, PA."

BLANCHE'S RESUME
ON REQUEST FROM STATUARY HALL

Blanche wrote a much less descriptive article for Statuary Hall when the "Architect of the Capitol" (the title of the director) in 1910 requested a brief biography. She wrote that she now "practiced little in public work principally because of the strain of the business part of it but has done a good deal privately, some at her own place and made models, etc., is a member of the Royal Arts of England, the Numismatic and Geographical Societies of New York." Nevin added a few telling lines: "I don't see what use all this is to anyone now— will that do? I do not care for notice." [32]*

---

*Author's note: Blanche was most recently and most completely written about in *Pioneering Sculptors*, a history of women working in three dimensions (1990).

NOTES ON PROPERTY
AT WINDSOR FORGE

Blanche's restoration of Windsor Forge began in 1899, and for some reason the deed was not recorded until 1913.

The beautiful doorway was done in Blanche's restoration, along with the semi-circular piazza with pillars at the back entrance. Blanche had one end of the piazza closed in with windows for a workroom-studio. The door opened on the porch, with no door inside, so the wall of the living room was not broken in its colonial design.

May 19, 1938

While Mrs. Davies, a cousin I believe, lived in Windsor Forge, she entertained the Pottstown historians for their "outing." Seventy-five members shared the historic experience as recorded by Francis Sayre in his autobiography, *Glad Adventure*.

May 3, 1995

The Iris Club Fine Arts Committee and a total of 45 members of the club were entertained with a tour of Windsor Forge. Carol Lux, present resident, gave the history as the women moved about the mansion and surveyed the back lawn to the Conestoga River. This is a private home, and we felt privileged to enter the beautiful doorway by special appointment. The author arranged the Iris Club visit to Windsor and the old Presbyterian Church built by Blanche's grandmother, Catherine Carmichael Jenkins, and we concluded with a visit to Old Bangor Church and graveyard, where the early Jenkinses are buried. Jerald Martin, president of the Caernarvon Historical Society, was our host in Churchtown, and aided Iris Club members in their search for ancestors' graves.

THE EIGHT-FOOT SANDSTONE TABLE TOP
FROM ROBERT SIMPSON'S ARTICLE

In 1907, Blanche decided she wanted a large stone table. It was to be eight feet in diameter and twenty inches thick from Turkey Hill quarry operated by Isaac Reifsnyder of Bowmansville. The estimated weight was eight tons, more than double the foot runner stones found in the local grist mills which weigh about 3,000 lbs.

The first two wagons carrying the stone collapsed. Later, a truck from United Traction Company of Reading was secured, and eight horses pulled it from the quarry to the lawn at Windsor.[12]

Each of the eight stone legs of the table were faced with sculpted faces of famous men. It was placed on the upper terrace near the semi-circular pillared porch.[12]

The accounts of the table's use indicate it was the centerpiece of Blanche's al Fresco entertaining.

Around 1959-60, the table disappeared. All eight tons of it are missing and no one seems to know what happened to the large disk. Later writers thought it was just a large millstone, but it far exceeded the size of the largest millstones.

The remains can be seen of the legs but the carved faces in clay are weathered away. The table should have stayed with Blanche's home.

BLANCHE THE PROTECTOR

Blanche was reported to assert herself in the interest of saving unsuspecting fish. If she saw people "gigging" at night in the Conestoga River, she would shoot her gun at them from her window.

Gigging fish was sort of like shooting sitting rabbits or deer at a salt lick, and has been illegal since the 1920s, when the law was passed.

The word was she knew how to use a gun. It is the only gun story that has been reported to the author.

CIVIL WAR CONNECTION

Blanche had two older brothers, Wilberforce and Robert Nevin who served in the Civil War, each attaining Captain rank. Robert requested a Colonelcy in a letter to Captain Cyrus S. Haldeman, but instead, his company was mustered out at Harrisburg soon after his request for promotion, and he went back to seminary.

Each May 30, Blanche entertained the Civil War Veterans for lunch around her huge table and back lawn area. I suspect this was her way of honoring her brothers' service. The picture is in the Earl Rebman book.

(See letters in appendix)

THE LAST KNOWN ROMANTIC
EVENT AT WINDSOR

On June 29, 1922, Margaret Lincoln and Clarkson Hunt were married at Windsor Forge. The small ceremony was held on the back lawn under the balcony. The bride's table was set on the front lawn with the Buddha sculpture as background. This was three years before Blanche died, and she was hosting the wedding of a second cousin. Blanche is in the wedding pictures.[5]

After the Francis Sayre-Jessie Wilson nuptials in the White House East Room, they toured Europe for their honeymoon, but did not think it complete until they spent several days at Windsor Forge, where they met.

And no wonder the visitors enjoyed Windsor Forge. The mansion's interior was decorated with Blanche's fine imported furniture, including a very ornate unusual carved cabinet desk. It was made of several woods. On her one wall hung her prized Venetian mirror, which was framed with etched mirrors and colored glass set in tin. Her own sculptures at this time were sitting around, with President McKinley and Theodore Roosevelt busts gracing the fireplace on either side, sitting on splendid dark marble pillars shaped at top and bottom. These are now at the Iris Club in the Nevin Room. They are dark brown marble with cream veining. The sculptures are somewhere else, location unknown.

In addition to her own art work, Blanche had brought back three large paintings purchased from an art dealer in Genoa, Italy. Miss Nevin believed them to be the work of Raphael DeMar. One was Joseph Interpreting Pharoah's Dream and one was Joseph with Potiphar's Wife. The third was not described. They were said to be from an abandoned Doge's Castle. Blanche's house was heated eventually with woodstoves and now, in 1995, has modern heating.

On the outside, the grounds were romantic. A walkway went down the center of the three terraces with pots of flowers along each side on the terrace level areas.

There were flower beds and, of course, the vine-covered sixty-foot pergola extending west of the house. Large shade trees added to the romantic ambiance and a trellis of vines ran down the west side of the terraces. Nothing was found to determine if they were grapes or flowering vines.

MRS. ULYSSES GRANT AT THE
CHICAGO EXPOSITION 1893

The persistence of Mrs. Grant's views is of interest to our times. Mrs. Grant was invited to view the show of women's work in their pavilion. The women had really put up a persistent vocal struggle to even be included in the fair.

Of course they were delighted to be permitted to have their own Women's Pavilion. They were told "Get up a side show for yourselves, pay for it yourselves, and be happy."[4]

It was with some dismay that the women heard the widowed Mrs. Grant's personal views during the preview reception:

"I do not approve of women sculptors or artists. The place of a woman is in the home looking to her husband's comfort and raising her children. They should be wives, mothers and housekeepers."[4] This was not what we would now call a "socially conscious" statement, and it only served to raise the ire of the women who had worked to have the pavilion and the artists whose work the pavilion displayed.

Some of the women at the fair were Mary Cassatt; Susan B. Anthony; Julia Ward Howe; Lucy Stone; Henrietta Szold, Jane Addams, Harriet Monroe; Frances Willard; Sarah Bernhardt; Clara Barton; Queen Victoria; Helena Modjeska; African Explorer, May French Sheldon; Sculptors Vinnie Ream Hoxie; Harriet Hosmer; and the architect Sophia Hayden.[4] These artists all had work to be judged, including Blanche Nevin.

March 4, 1885, Ottawa, Canada

At some point, Blanche had taken a pen name, Bianca.

BIANCA IN CANADA
Ottawa, February 23, 1885

"Prescott is an old fashioned town, where our baggage is examined. Houses are generally built of stone. There I began to notice the nice fur overcoats for the men. They look extremely picturesque, particularly those worn by the coachmen. They are silvery gray."

Blanche's (Bianca's) correspondence columns told of fashions and the personalities of the people, now considered human interest.

Poems were often written on complimentary stationery when traveling. *Coptic* and *Doric* were two of the steamship names. Bianca jotted down the inscription a friend told her was on a tombstone in the West. Perhaps it struck a cord of thought for herself. "She done what she could."

BLANCHE'S MATERNAL GRANDMOTHER

This lady was eulogized in a book about her life. Catherine Carmichael Jenkins, Mrs. Robert, was orphaned at an age of about 11 years. Her father, a minister, had been widowed by Catherine's birth.

At his deathbed, when deciding where his several children should live, he ran out of places and said, "Catherine, I will give her to the Lord."

She lived with one minister's family and it appears three different families in all before her marriage to Robert Jenkins.

Their home at Windsor became a way station for itinerant ministers, and she lived what she felt was a devoted life, raising the family that is noted elsewhere, and always proselytizing to others.

Two stories about her were probably passed on quite readily as good examples, since she did not allow card playing or wine parties in her home.

When they lived in Washington during Robert's term in Congress during Jefferson and Madison's Presidencies, she did not falter in her belief. In fact, she is recorded as having approached President Jefferson at a levee, a reception usually in someone's honor. One of the other ladies commented on the sermon several had heard the previous Sunday with a topic, "God is Love." The lady speaking seemed to consider that discourse rather inferior since she thought it inappropriate, considering the text from which it was taken. She was trying to indicate to President Jefferson that she too was a skeptic and had renounced all belief in Divine revelation as he had. She inquired how the President liked the discourse (sermon). He replied, "Oh, ladies are fond of the subject of love, and, of course, I approve the subject," with a significant smile.

Catherine Jenkins felt that her duty to her Heavenly Father forbade her to be silent. She felt called upon to defend the Sacred Word.

She replied to the president. She expressed her views and feelings on the subject of God's love and his revelation to our fallen world with respect to the person she addressed. Her remarks were followed by an expressive silence, and she felt gratification that in the halls of Washington, a humble but decided follower of Christ could gain access to the conscience." [59]

Another not so "socially conscious" person in interpreting the silence.

The other of several stories is along similar lines but involved General Lafayette when he traveled the United States.* In the autumn of 1824, Lafayette was invited to Lancaster, Pennsylvania to visit and to witness the baptism of a child named for him. One of the prominent citizens in Lancaster was George B. Porter, Esq., who was Attorney General of Pennsylvania, and afterward Governor of the Michigan territory appointed by President Andrew Jackson.[59]

This was the child of Sara Humes Porter and George. Sara is credited with building the house in 1858 on Duke Street now owned by The Iris Club. It was purchased in 1898 for $14,500 after having at least three owners. The Iris Club was organized by Blanche's sister, Alice.

Mrs. Catherine Jenkins was among the guests at the christening of Lafayette Porter, the infant. She seized the occasion for opening a conversation with the Marquis de Lafayette on the subject of church and the cause of Christ. Lafayette expressed his gratification at witnessing the baptism, of its solemnity and simplicity, as being in accordance with his views of the spirit of true Christianity. He expressed his admiration for the clergy of the country; of their high moral influences; and of their patriotism during the Revolutionary War.

Mrs. Jenkins replied she was the daughter of a Presbyterian clergyman, who had taken a very ardent and active stand in the cause of liberty and who had occasion to be in communication with General Washington.[59]

Mrs. Jenkins' father's communication with General Washington had to do with the great need for supplies for the troops at Valley Forge. From his pulpit he was asking for everything warm and preserved food that could be spared by parishioners. It was then transported in some fashion to the post at Valley Forge. Robert Simpson reported having seen a letter with Washington's signature as a youth.

Mrs. Jenkins' stories are included to give some ancestral perspective from which Blanche grew.

When thinking of Blanche, these stories emphasized that having one's own beliefs and standards were admired. Blanche knew this grandmother and doubtless heard the stories told often.

That Blanche had well-developed creativity was evident in her writings, her home, and sculpture production.

The lex pax carved in her mantle in 1925 indicates her wish to live the "law of peace." Blanche experienced the Civil War.

---

*In the biography of Catherine Jenkins, Rev. Lehman wrote that Catherine's father had received threats that the British were looking for him due to sending or taking supplies to Washington at Valley Forge.

LATE IN THE ARTIST'S LIFE

A Mr. Martin did odd jobs for Blanche and knew her well in her last years. He too has died. But one record was found that he would bring heated water to Blanche's bedroom at bedtime and sit in the hall until she was finished bathing and would clear the bath things away and lock up before he left for the night to go home to his wife.

The stories of Blanche having men around may have stemmed from this or the fact that to keep Windsor Forge beautiful, there needed to be manual labor done at regular intervals. She heated with woodstoves and cooked with wood. The Hannah that is mentioned in the poem "One Usual Day" was evidently the housekeeper.

BLANCHE AND HER MOTHER

A note from Alice, Blanche's sister, to Elias Davis, Esquire, family Boonsboro, MD, in 1888.

"My mother and Blanche are at Atlantic city spending a week or so. Ma has failed very visibly this spring and we thought the change would do her good. They were there during the dreadful storm and I was very uneasy lest they suffer from it.

With kind regards to Mrs. Davis and Miss Carrie. Believe me.

Yours very sincerely,

Alice Nevin"[5]

Those who have said Blanche was not close to her family were not aware of all the comings and goings of Blanche. Especially after she left Lancaster to study in Philadelphia. Several incidents of family togetherness have been cited to lay that belief of uninvolvment to rest.

FINDING BLANCHE'S HISTORY

According to the Farmers Trust Company history[41] (1810-1910), in the article about Blanche's Uncle William Jenkins, Esq., who was the third president of the company and prosecuting attorney for twenty-three years,* Blanche is noted as being the owner of part of the once vast estate, including "the ancient and picturesque mansion."

A side historic note is that he built and resided in Wheatland on the Marietta turnpike. This estate was afterwards acquired by Hon. William M. Meredith of Philadelphia, one of the country's greatest lawyers who sold it to President James Buchanan in 1848.

Mr. William Jenkins died in this city on May 24, 1853.[41]

---

*The prosecuting attorney then was appointed by Governor Findley in 1817.

MORE ANECDOTAL INFORMATION

Blanche's sister, Alice, had a student, Perry Smith, living with her. His room was free for working around the place, on Lancaster Avenue. He is the one person who seems to have said "Blanche was a drinker" because she would come to Alice's and seem loud to him. *Maybe* Perry was being checked on to see if he was working his share. At any rate, he doesn't sound like he cared for Blanche at all.

He and Foxy Heller, who lived across the street from Alice, both seemed to be a bit of a gossip and had a low tolerance for difference in people.

Foxy told of a time when Blanche was in Penn Square with another woman, wearing her "atrocious purple hat" and people were staring at her. Perhaps people recognized her as the noted sculptress who had family in town. Blanche was always the individual, and contrary to her note to Statuary Hall that she didn't want notice, she seemed to seek it in socially acceptable ways, as most middle children do, in just about everything she did. Perry Smith was also bothered by Blanche's long serpent necklace and he remarked on how she kept pointing the snake's head at him as she talked. I suppose this could be intimidating, but whether it was a constant activity is not known. Others remember hearing of her serpent necklace, no doubt a souvenir of one of her trips.

THE HAUNTED ROOM

It became a mystery of some proportion when Blanche continually found her bed cover folded back. Day after day they listened and watched. When she would go to her room, the cover was folded back again. This puzzlement about who could be haunting Windsor went on for some time.

Finally, one day a gust of wind blew through the window and someone saw the cover blown back. Her bed was sitting between two open windows. Some have said she slept in her big old king's bed on the third floor.

Carol Lux, present resident, says with a secretive smile that they still think it is haunted at times. They hear different sounds. Who could it be? The only violent sudden death that I read about was Blanche's uncle John, who died in an accident at one of the forges. The Luxes like to think it is Blanche.

MORE ABOUT THE FORGE DAYS

As you remember, John Jenkins sold his 400 acres after nine years and building the stone block house, to William Branson, who took his sons-in-law, Lynford Lardner, Samuel Flower, and Richard Hockley as partners, and they continued the forge business for thirty years. At that time there were five forges and 3,000 acres.

David Jenkins, John's son, had been in their employ moving up to bookkeeper. In 1773, when Lardner's wife died, David bought her shares. Prior to the Revolutionary War in 1775 to 1783, he had secured the whole property for approximately 5,000 pounds for the total.

David continued the forge business, losing one brother in a forge accident, until 1800 when his son Robert Jenkins assumed full charge.

During the Revolutionary War, the forges cooperated with Grubb mines at Cornwall and the early DuPont plant, which made gun powder along the Brandywine River.

THE STOLEN LION STORY

During the late 1970s, the lion on the left as you approach the front door of Windsor Forge was broken from its pedestal and stolen.

Newspaper articles asked for its return and described the lion and its history. After several months, a policeman saw something different in the medial strip of a local highway.

When he saw the lion he remembered the description, and the lion was returned to Windsor Forge. Fortunately, it was not badly broken and is again in his rightful place, opposite his twin at the entrance of Windsor as Blanche had placed them.

Unfortunately, the large disk of her stone table has not been found or returned.

ATTEMPT TO ADOPT A WAIF

Blanche was travelling in poor but scenic country, and wrote down her feelings about eating so many courses of food in front of a little boy waif standing outside the window. Upon leaving the restaurant, she sought the boy and talked with him and then with others who knew him. He was reported to not know a father and his mother put him out because he wasn't bringing enough money home from begging. Blanche asked the boy about coming to the United States with her and living with her. It progressed so that she went before a committee of ruling men in the town and was told she was being "taken" because the boy and his friends just wanted her to give money. They also asked, in deprecatory manner, why a lone woman would want to adopt a waif, refusing her petition.

When Blanche next wrote, she was still working out her disappointment, and still did not quite see why her wish to help the waif was denied (see next page).

Author's Note

This is an incomplete self-analysis that came about because Blanche had been rebuked for trying to help a waif. It fostered her growth of even stronger feminist beliefs than she already held.

THE NEW YORK 7 PUERTO RICO STEAMSHIP COMPANY
ON BOARD *S. S. CAROLINA*

[Sheet 1]

I thought I had considered it all, and that there was little responsibility in picking up a waif and wrapping[?] the mantle of protection about him. It would have been a matter for hesitancy if it was taking him away from an assured position. He hadn't *any*. No father, an unwilling mother—and an accumulating record against him in the police books. The prospect of his future was threatening and likely to smother out any inclination to right or good in him. Association of a boy of ten with criminals is not the best school to aid development.

And here were the men all dividing and opposing the idea. Well fed men more or less successful in life. Well dressed, comfortable, and shrewd. Their attitude was depress[ing?] and [weakening?] [second sheet]—was I possibly a fool? an "impulsive feminine (Oh damning word) creature," impractical, visionary, kindly meaning but a flabby fool. Didn't they know better than I did? Their contact with the affairs of life had been greater, broader. I had simply laid myself open to a broadside of deserved fire from these superior and knowing beings—been impulsive—

A little thought crept in, "Why is it not right to be impulsive if the impulse and [heat?] of it comes from love of [..?..] and right, and [...?...] with injustice?"

But it was a little thought one hardly let grow or nourish. In endeavoring to accord and harmonize ourselves into prevalent modes of thought and action one must really quite smother some [presenting?]

thoughts. "Get thee behind me—etc."

[third sheet:] The heart without impulse—is it not gristle? The cold heart can be warmed—but gristle [?] take [heat? heart?] It says[?]—gristle says "Why are you not like me, superior to these outbursts of illy regulated feeling? Learn to be gentle and [superior?]. You will wear yourself out. The continual [importancing?] of the mere self. As if life wouldn't go on without us.

[fourth sheet:] But we women have so much that has been taught us to unlearn [before?] if we would be of use to God and humanity— we are taught to distrust our own judgement—to subordinate it to that of others—male others. It is a slow process to get rid of timorousness when we do take independent action and keep steady heads when firm decision is needed against odds.

[fifth sheet] Then in making decisions one is hounded by the sense of being a woman. Church and Law have rubbed it into us— with salt—that we are inferior to the male—and deliberately taught self distrust. And they also have much to unlearn. To do them justice there is no doubt some of them really believe it. Church and State have taught them so. All [minds?] are not elastic. The slothful continue in [?].

VISIT TO COAMO SPRINGS, PUERTO RICO
April 1, 1909

Blanche wrote special correspondence for the NEW ERA about her visit to Coamo Springs, Puerto Rico. The Springs were likened to the Newport or Saratoga spas of the States.

Her comparison of Coamo Spring water with others goes like this, "the water is sulphur, but not so much as in Ceasar's favorite spring at Le Prese, where the air is full of smell. It is also hot, but less so than at the Japanese springs at Atami, where it fumes and bubbles violently that it throws into the air at times a jet or fountain quite high."

WINTERTIME IN VENICE

Blanche wrote of the year-round residents of Venice and how different Venice was without crowds of tourists when she chose to vacation this time.

"'Edolce for mente," "It is sweet to do nothing," was a timeless slogan for vacationing. But Venice evidently was having a cold winter. Her description of how the poor old women use scaldini, little earthen bowls with handles like baskets, that are filled with one or two cents' worth of charcoal: "Scaldini are not so bad if you have nothing better. You nurse them on your lap crouching over them, and poke with sticks and blow on them so that the coals are alive again."

WINDSOR FORGE AND POOLE FORGE

Because of confusion about ownership among today's history buffs, this little attempt at elucidation may help in understanding the Windsor and Poole Forge connection, which basically there was little.

Davies sold land to Windsor and to Poole Forge.

Old, who created Poole Forge, had worked earlier as a puddler at Windsor Forge. He later worked at Poole, then built Speedwell Forge, and later bought Quitahilla Forge, West of Lebanon.

Windsor and Poole were never a joint business venture as I have found the history. If this is in error, another historian can get it clear.

BLAIR STATUE COMPETITION
June 23, 1881

A newspaper article in Philadelphia reported the following: "Yesterday morning the model for the Blair statue, which has so long been expected from Miss Blanche Nevin of Lancaster, Pennsylvania, arrived in this city and was set up with the others in the Art Gallery of Messrs. Pettes and Leathe, where it is now on exhibition. It was shipped on the 10th of May from Massa de Carrara, Italy, where Miss Nevin has been residing for some time."

This was the only time the Blair statue was mentioned as one of Blanche's sculptures. Later, a columnist reported the awarding of the Commission to a gentleman known by many of the committee. Where Blanche's entry is now not found in this search, it is clear that Blanche was actively pursuing her career of sculpture, and one is led to believe that there are more works of Blanche "out there" than we have knowledge of, and it has not helped that she did not sign some of her work.

100 YEAR OLD ALVIN WEAVER REMEMBERS BLANCHE

Alvin Weaver was born in 1896 on a farm near Windsor Forges. He became the mail carrier for Blanche, trudging up the hill to the Churchtown post office twice a day. He would sling the tooled Mexican leather mail bag over his shoulder and bring Blanche's mail himself. He remembers her mail very well.

When he was nine years old, he watched the sculpting of the lion prototype as it progressed on the front lawn at Windsor Forge. He said it was quite a new experience for a wide-eyed boy.

In 1918-1920, when Alvin was a newly married man, he was Blanche's chauffeur, driving her all about—to Manasquan, Sea Girt, New Jersey, and to Bethlehem to see Patty, her younger sister. Blanche's car was an Overland, a prestigious car of the times.

Alvin's friend Sam Shirk drove Blanche to Miami, Florida one winter. They stayed about two months and as Mr. Weaver said, "They were in separate quarters, of course, but Blanche footed the bill." This is probably the same "Shirk" mentioned in a poem.

When Blanche entertained the Civil War Veterans each Memorial Day, Alvin ground the coffee beans many times for the picnics. He also remembered that the housekeeper's last full name was Hannah Frankhouser. He also told stories of how Blanche spent one whole summer touring around the Meditteranean and Egypt.

Mr. Weaver admired Blanche for restoring Windsor Forges Mansion, he found her to have a nice personality, but he also noted that she liked things to be a certain way—it was her nature.

---

*Alvin Weaver came to the author's attention in a newspaper article celebrating his century of living. We spoke for about an hour.

Appendix

*Letter to Blanche Nevin from her father, John W. Nevin. Blanche
was 21 years old.*

Lancaster, November 15, 1962

My dear daughter,

We were glad to hear that you have got settled in your new quarters and fully engaged in your studies. By this time I trust you have gotten over any touches of homesickness and feel yourself morally acclimated to your change of circumstances. There is nothing like regular and full employment to make the mind contented; as nothing is more favorable to dyspepsia and ennui than the feeling of having nothing to do.

Still you must not task your powers too much in the way of mental application lest they give way and you fail altogether. Do not undertake, either in drawing or French, more than you can get along with comfortably, under the idea of saving time and money. As regards to your studies and drawing in particular I do not wish you to place yourself under any inconvenient situations. If you find that your taste and talents are such as to freely justify the application of yourself in this way, I am quite willing that you should have the opportunity of doing so to any reasonable extent; even so far indeed, if you desire it as your taking the full course of the instruction you are now attending. Especially so if it should promise to give you the power of providing for yourself in the world. Whatever may serve that purpose, is of course worth what it may cost; since no money can ever be of the same value to us as the probity of independence lodged in our own persons.

Alice had a letter the other day from Wilberforce, dated in the neighborhood of Bowling Green, and reporting him in good health. From Robert we have not heard since you left. I live in continued concern for their welfare but try to hope that through the great goodness of God, all may come out right with regard to them in the end. They should be the subject of our continual prayers. [Wilberforce and Robert were already in the army of the North before the Civil War.]

The work of organizing and officering the new drafted regiment, after much confusion, seemed now to be going forward in Harrisburg; but I am afraid that there is not much chance of appointment for Will. There is too much selfish management and political wireworking for any measure of proposition to succeed simply on the strength of its merits. It was published that the appointments to field officer would be made in general only from such as have been in actual war service for a year. But I see that the selections for Lancaster County regiment are not of this character at all; and so it will go probably with the appointments in general.

You must not forget to call, some time, on the family of your cousin Charlie Reynolds. They would be hurt if you would be in the city any time without making them a visit.

You need not be particular about attending Dr. Bomberger's church, unless it may happen to suit your taste. If the family with which you are boarding attend where there are edifying services, it may be as well to fall in for the time with their worship.

In any case make conscience of cultivating the spirit of religion in sincerity and truth. All else for us in this world is uncertain of comparative small account. If there be any reality at all in the gospel of Christ it is of such unutterably momentous interest that it must ever be the height of folly not to give it our whole heart or to make it in any way of interest of only secondary regard. And every year you live now you will find that you need, more and more, its consolation and support; for the further we enter into the experience of our present life the more certainly do we find it to be labor and sorrow, vanity and vexation of spirit.

> With love from all the family,
> Your affectionate father,
> J. W. Nevin

Lancaster, June 28, 1863

My dear daughter,

It is a great relief now that you and our cousins Effie and Emily are out of the way. The "scare" after days ago is terrible earnest today. You will be able to see by the papers but may wish also a line from home.

The enemy is but a short way from Harrisburg. We have been listening for commencement of a battle there all day, but it has not come. In the meantime, a force is moving toward the river at York, which may reach Columbia before morning. While I write the bridge at Columbia is on fire; and the smoke can be seen from this place. [Caernarvon Place, their home]

Lancaster is in great commotion. People are packing up goods to send off.

Robert has his battery completed and is ordered to Harrisburg tomorrow. Cecil remains at home. The rest of us also mean to sit still and take things as they come.

It is reported that Hooker and Picket, have got as far as to Peach Bottom; some 6,000 troops of General Dix are expected to pass through here tonight for Columbia.

Letters from Pittsburgh announce the death of Mr. Irwin, father-in-law of your uncles Daniel and Theodore [Nevin].

Miss Lane and Miss Annie Buchanan came up to Wheatland yesterday. Miss Lane wishes to remain with her uncle, but he refuses to hear anything of the sort and insists on her prompt departure again.

I write at your uncle Williams; finding Mattie has a letter for Alice written yesterday. I enclose it in the same envelope.

We are in the hands of God. He can make all things work for good in the end. I am of course greatly concerned for Robert; but he is in the way of duty.

Since I commenced writing we have word that a train was fired on across the river between this and Harrisburg this afternoon; but no injury was done.

Thus you have all our latest news. Your mother was sick yesterday and in the doctor's hands; but she is better today again and will be up and about, I trust, tomorrow. She bears the exciting occasion now upon us with proper calmness.

Mr. Buchanan with his two nieces came round to see us on their way from church.

We are entering on a very solemn night and tomorrow may bring sobering things. There must be fighting soon, perhaps at different points. Love to all our friends.

Your affectionate father,
J. W. Nevin

Alice had been ill after a heart attack, so that may account for Blanche's funeral being from Alice's house. Blanche had been staying at the Brunswick to look after Alice.

August 25, 1939

Mrs. Lindsay Patterson
Long Hope Hill
Russellville, Tenn.

My dear Mrs. Patterson:

My brother has asked me to answer your inquiry of August 10th about my aunt, Miss Blanche Nevin.

Miss Nevin died in the Lancaster General Hospital at Lancaster, PA. on April 21, 1925. I was with her at the time. She was eighty-three years old; her death was mainly due to natural infirmities coupled with heart trouble. We had a private room at the hospital and, as nearly as I remember, she had been there for something like ten days. She was buried from the home of her sister, Miss Alice Nevin and interred in the Woodward Hill Cemetery of Lancaster, in the Nevin family lot. The inscription which my brother and I chose for her tombstone was taken from one of her verses:

> "Now will I pray
> Not for the dower
> Of beauty, grace or brilliant power
> But that the gift of kindness may
> Descend, possess and with me stay."

The old family home at Windsor Forges, where she used to live, is now in my possession.

I do not know that there is anything else very much which I can tell you. Up to almost the end Miss Nevin was her unique, natural and fascinating self.

Yours sincerely,
John Nevin Sayre

JNS:et
c. Francis B. Sayre

REPORT OF STATUARY COMMISSION TO SENATE
January 9, 1879

Mr. Daniel Ermentrout presented the report of the statuary commission, which was read as follows, viz:

"To the honorable Senate and House of Representatives of the Commonwealth of Pennsylvania:

"The commission appointed by the Governor of Pennsylvania, under an act 'providing for a commission to have statues executed and placed in the old hall of the House of Representatives in the capitol of the United States, and making an appropriation therefor,' approved the 18th day of April, 1877, in pursuance of its fourth section, directing an annual report to the Legislature of the progress in the work contemplated by said act, beg leave to submit the following report:

"The commission composed of Simon Cameron, of Harrisburg; Daniel Ermentrout, of Reading; John C. Hager, of Lancaster; Thomas MacKennan of Washington; Francis A. Osbourn, and George DeB. Keim, of Philadelphia, met at the call of the Governor, in pursuance of said act, in the office of the Secretary of the Commonwealth, in Harrisburg, on the 18th day of October, 1877, and after being duly sworn by the Secretary to perform their duties with fidelity, effected an organization by the election of Simon Cameron, as president, and George deB. Keim, as secretary of the commission.

"On the 19th day of January, 1878, the commission met at the hall of the Historical Society of Pennsylvania, in Philadelphia; on the 22nd of February, at the capitol of the United States at Washington, and on the 11th of April, at Lancaster, when General Peter Muhlenberg and

Robert Fulton were selected as subjects for the statues.

"On the 31st day of May, the commission met at Reading, and decided that the statues should be of marble; on the 10th of August, they met at Atlantic City; on the 21st of August, at Philadelphia; on the 10th of October, at Donegal, and on the 7th of November, at the Pennsylvania Academy of the Fine Arts, at Philadelphia, when Miss Blanche Nevin, of Lancaster, was selected to execute the statue of General Peter Muhlenberg, and Howard Roberts, of Philadelphia, that of Robert Fulton, in marble, for the price of $7,500 each.

"On the 18th of December, the commission met in Philadelphia, when the contracts were entered into with the artists—copies of which are hereto annexed and submitted.

"The commission respectfully suggests to your honorable bodies, that an appropriation will now be necessary, in accordance with the terms of the contracts.

"By section third, the sum of two thousand dollars was appropriated for the purposes named in the act, and the traveling expenses of the commission, of which sum no part has yet been expended."

SIMON CAMERON
President.

GEORGE DeB. KEIM,
Secretary[32]

Blanche Nevin's contract with the State of Pennsylvania for the Muhlenberg Statue she sculpted for Statuary Hall in Washington

Contract entered into this eighteenth day of December, AD Eighteen Hundred and Seventy Eight, between Blanche Nevin of the first part, Simon Cameron, President, Daniel Ermentrout, John C. Hager, Thomas McKennan, Francis A. Osbourne, and George DeB. Kerin, Secretary, Commissioners, constituted and appointed by and under an Act of the General Assembly of the Commonwealth of Pennsylvania entitled "An Act providing for a Commission to have statues executed and placed in the Old Hall of the House of Representatives in the Capitol of the United States and making an appropriation therefore approved April 18, 1877, of the second part.

Witnesseth that the party of the first part in consideration of the sum of Seven Thousand Five Hundred dollars to be paid to her hereinafter mentioned, agrees to make for said Commonwealth a statue of General Peter Muhlenberg of the first quality of Carrara statuary marble and of heroic size, and in two years from the date of this contract to place and set up the said statue complete in all respects, upon a pedestal of suitable proportions, of proper design, and of the very best marble and workmanship, in the old Hall of the House of Representatives in the Capitol of the United States, which is set apart as a national statuary hall. For which statue and pedestal and all expenses connected therewith, including the cost of transportation and setting up thereof, the party of the first part shall receive the said sum of money from the said Commonwealth as follows: On the completion of the model of the statue, the sum of three thousand seven hundred and fifty dollars, and on the completion, placing and setting up the statue, the further and final sum of three thousand seven hundred and fifty dollars, which shall be in full payment for said statue and pedestal and all expenses connected therewith, including the transportation and setting up thereof.

And it is further understood and agreed by the party of the first part that the parties of the second part, each and every of them, constituted and appointed and herein acting under and by virtue of the Act of Assembly herein before mentioned and empowered by the same to select artists and contract for the execution of two statues for said Commonwealth, are to occupy individually or collectively, towards the party of the first part, no position directly or indirectly, of pecuniary responsibility for the work to be done by the party of the first part under this contract, but that they, the party of the second part, contract and act herein only in a fiduciary capacity and as agents for the Commowealth of Pennsylvania.

In witness whereof the parties of the first and second parts have here-unto subscribed their names the day and year above written (the words Blanche Nevin, her and General Peter Muhlenberg being first interlined).

Blanche's Writing at 81 Years

Souvenir of the Pilgramage
or
The Historical Society of Berks County
to
Windsor Forges
(1742)
in
Caernarvon Township, Lancaster County,
Pennsylvania

September 2, 1921

Presented by Miss Blanche Nevin

DEDICATED TO
THE GHOSTS OF WINDSOR FORGES
POLITELY
BY THEIR PRESENT PROPRIETOR
BLANCHE NEVIN

TO MY DOOR
By: Miss Blanche Nevin

If genius, or the studious brain
By happy chance, should kindly deign
To tap upon thy wooden side,
Open, my door, fly open wide.

To gentle courtesy, to grace,
To wit, good heart, and smiling face;
To the frank brow, the honest hand,
Open, my door, wide open stand.

To love, to friendship and to truth,
To interesting age, or youth;
To worthy rich or worthy poor,
Stand ever open wide, my door.

If formal folk would visit make
Receive them for politeness sake;
But to the stupid or the bore
Creak slowly on thy hinge, my door.

If fate unkind should ever send
Hypocrisy in guise of friend,
If insincerity should knock
Tighten thy lock, tighten thy lock.

Strengthen thy bolts against the bad,
Keep out the snob, keep out the cad,
And all impurity and sin,
But let the tired and patient in.

Shams, pomps, pain, the Devil
Himself, and all his imps of evil,

If they should dare to prowl about,
Put up thy bar, and keep them out.

And when some day, with solemn face,
Winged Azrael shall cleave through space,
Hither to bear my soul away,
Usher him in without delay.

BLANCHE NEVIN

THE STORY OF WINDSOR FORGES

On December 28, 1742, William Branson acquired a patent for a tract of land which loyally he called "Windsor," after the King's palace in England. During this year he built a forge on the Conestoga, a short distance below the site on which, shortly after, he erected his mansion house, which is now the eastern part of the present building. The western end and larger part was built in 1765. Later, another forge was built to the east of the mansion house, near the dam at the road.

Branson conducted many operations and associated with him his four sons-in-law, Samuel Flower, Richard Hockley, Lynford Lardner and Bernard Van Leer, to all of whom by deed dated December 14, 1754, he transferred all of his property, including of course "Windsor Forges." Lynford Lardner's sister was married to Richard Penn, and he himself occupied different positions of trust and authority in the Colonial government. He appears to have been the active manager and the most active of the sons-in-law in the business. He instituted the Assemblies in Philadelphia, and also lived at "Windsor" and without doubt brought some of the Colonial social life from Philadelphia to this place.

Amongst the early settlers in the great Valley in Chester County, in 1700, came David Jenkins from Wales. Following a family custom, his eldest son was called after the grandfather—John. And this John Jenkins became the pioneer of the family in this Conestoga Valley. He received some lands by patent and bought others, including a part of the Gabriel Davies patent which lay to the east of Windsor.

John Jenkin's wife was Aurelia (which she changed to Rebecca when she left the Episcopal Church to become a Quaker) Meredith, daughter of Sarah Aurelia Rush,

"...grandchild of Colonel Rush, who fled,
After the roundheads cut off King Charles' head.
Of Cromwell's army, he, of stubborn faith,
Whose daughter—so the ancient Bible saith,
Was the first white girl born of Englishment
Within the settlement of William Penn."

A son of this John Jenkins and Rebecca Meredith Jenkins, by name David Jenkins (after his grandfather) in 1773, married Martha Armour, daughter of General Robert Armour of Pequea, of Scotch-Irish ancestry, and a valiant soul—

"Martha Armour. She who put to flight
And foiled by strategy the Doanes one night.
*   *   *   *   *   *
Coming one day from harvesting the hay
Men found her by the old well, where she lay,
In a dead faint, her baby in her arms,
Held tight, and screaming, full of vague alarms.
They 'brought her to,'
But all she knew was that she saw her child
Fall in the well. Then she went wild;
This told she remembered, nothing more.
But both were wringing wet, and bruised and sore.
How she got up, none knew. "Twas thought
Climbing, the baby in her teeth, was brought."

This David Jenkins had been for thirty years with the Company of Branson's sons-in-law, and the same year in which he was married he bought a half interest, and subsequently the remaining part of the property, including the negro slaves and stock. He was a member of the Provincial Convention in 1775 and 1776 and served on numerous patriotic committees during the Revolutionary War, besides being Colonel of the Tenth Battalion of Lancaster County Militia, which he recruited and equipped. He operated these works, and the farms which took the place of the forests after they were cleared, until his death in 1797. His eldest son, following the family custom, was called John and assisted in the conduct of the forges and business until his early death, the result of an accident. Windsor, with the three thousand acres which had been added to the property, together with an acre of land in West Nantmeall Township in Chester County, "in which said acre there is contained a body of Iron Ore," David Jenkins then devised to another son Robert Jenkins who became the Iron Master here. Another son, William Jenkins, became a member of the Lancaster Bar; built "Wheatland"—later President Buchanan's home; was married to Mary Hubley, whose granddaughter became Baroness De Reuter, and is now the widow of James Gordon Bennett.

Robert Jenkins was married to Catharine Mustard Carmichael, whose life and history add a most exquisite charm as well as interesting romance to even fascinating Windsor. Her father, whose mother was a niece of the Duke of Argyle, as a boy in crossing the ocean in 1737 from Scotland to New York, had been swept or jolted from the ship into the ocean, to be providentially rescued. Subsequently, he dedicated his life to God and was graduated from Princeton in 1759. He was ordained and installed pastor of the Presbyterian Church at the Forks of the Brandywine in Chester County. His second wife was Catharine Mustard, who died after the birth (on July 23, 1774) of her daughter Catharine. Rev. Carmichael was an intense patriot during the war, an eloquent preacher, and a God-fearing parent of a large family. On his death bed, after bestowing his blessing upon his children and providing for the care of his other children, he pondered long as to whom he should give Catharine. After a few minutes' pause, he said, "I give her to the Lord." This young girl possessed unusual charm and intelligence and resided as a daughter with the family of Daniel Buckley at Buckley's forge. The gallant, young and attractive Iron Master at Windsor met this "charge of God" and they were married in September 1799, shortly after he had inherited Windsor. Upon becoming Lady of the Manor and helpmeet to its Master, whether we remember him as Iron Master, farmer, member of the State

Legislature or as Congressman. Beautiful, of stern Presbyterian convictions and a strong personality, and most charitable, she possessed a culture that was unusually captivating and charming, whether manifested amongst the tenants and laborers of this place or its neighbors; at the inaugural ball of President Jefferson; at a reception to Lafayette where she held a long conversation with him; or in meeting the learned and pious to whom Windsor became a most congenial stopping place.

The life and character of Robert Jenkins and his wife may well be indicated by naming some of their children and their descendants.

1. David Jenkins, the eldest son, a Princeton graduate, who had operated the works with his father, and by whom (his father having increased the ancestral holdings by a thousand acres to four thousand acres) Windsor with its forges and land were accepted after the death of the father in 1848 at a value of nearly $60,000. David enjoyed his sole proprietorship only a few years, for he died May 22, 1850, a bachelor:

"Urbane in his manners, classic in his taste, refined in his feelings, a Christian in his principles. He was in life highly esteemed and tenderly beloved, and in death deeply and painfully lamented."(Epitaph.)

2. Elizabeth Jenkins, the eldest daughter, married Phillip Wager Reigart, of an old Lancaster family. She acquired title to the lower forge and the Windsor Mansion in partition proceedings in her brother's estate on March 16, 1857. During her ownership the forge was operated for some time by Jacob Mentzer of Pottstown and after 1868 James McCaa operated it for two years. Wm. J. McCaa, Esq., a grandson of David Jenkins, operated it last.

Mrs. Reigart conveyed the mansion and about 87 acres surrounding it to her daughter, Catharine R. Cummins, who in turn in 1899 conveyed it with 34 acres 72 perches to Miss Blanche Nevin.

3. Martha Jenkins, married to Dr. John W. Nevin, Presbyterian Minister, who became the leading Theologian of the Reformed Church at Mercersburg and Lancaster; President of Franklin and Marshall College.

Their children included William Wilberforce Nevin, lawyer, Captain through the Civil War, Adjutant General on General Granger's staff; aided in the construction of the Denver & Rio Grande Railroad, was sometime editor of the *Philadelphia Press*; Rev. Robert Jenkins Nevin, D.D., leaving his studies at the seminary to become Captain of a battery in the Civil War, where he had a brilliant record. Clergyman in the Episcopal Church and builder of the first Protestant Episcopal Church in Rome, where he served until his death, extensive traveler, cosmopolitan, an authority on antiques and connoisseur of art, buried at Arlington; Miss Alice Nevin, the founder and first president of the Iris Club at Lancaster, composer of hymns, a leader in the intellectual, social, civic and charitable life of Lancaster, to whose genius many of its organizations owe their existence; Martha Nevin, married to Robert Sayre, whose two sons are Rev. John Nevin Sayre, an Episcopalian clergyman, now secretary of the International Society of Reconciliation, and Francis Bowes Sayre, lawyer, professor of International Law at Harvard, author of various books and pamphlets, married to Jessie, daughter of Woodrow Wilson, and father of three children in the ninth generation in the Jenkins family in America; Miss Blanche Nevin, sculptor of versatility, traveler, cosmopolitan, whose artistic sense and unusual originality enliven a most fascinating conversationalist, who brings a golden era to dear old Windsor.

The world she knows so thoroughly,
From Old Cairo to far Hong Kong,
From Manasquan to quaint Churchtown.

4. Phoebe Ann Jenkins, married to Rev. John W. Scott, president of Washington and Jefferson College.

5. Catharine Jenkins, married to General Hanson Bentley Jacobs, of Churchtown, who was a descendant of Cyrus Jacobs of "Spring Grove Forge." She accepted title to the upper Windsor Forge property upon the death of her son David.

6. Mary Jenkins, married to Rev. William W. Latta, pastor of the Presbyterian Church of Waynesburgh, now Honey Brook, Pa.

7. Sarah Jenkins, married to Rev. Alfred Nevin, D.D., a Presbyterian Minister, a cousin of Dr. John W. Nevin.

8. Dr. John Carmichael Jenkins, graduate of Dickinson College, who inherited the large Carmichael Estate in Mississippi, where he moved and where he heroically lost his life while ministering to his patients during an epidemic of cholera. He left a large and interesting family of descendants.

Mrs. Robert Jenkins died on September 23, 1856, and with her death the old glory of Windsor Forges departed. The life and character of the place became commonplace and uninteresting. The various forges in the vicinity, Windsor, Poole, Spring Grove, secured their charcoal iron from Elizabeth, Warwick, Hopewell, or Joanna Furnaces. No ore was discovered in this vicinity until the late fifties, when small mines were opened from which the ore was taken to Birdsboro or Joanna and the iron was brought back to these forges. High costs, lack of railroad facilities and lumber, made it impossible for these water-power forges to compete with the more modern mills. A century and a quarter were required for the making of charcoal iron "the morning glory of American industry," to run its course, and the famous combination of the products of the woods, quarries, mines, and labor yielded only to the inevitable progress of a wonderful and interesting industry.

The glow of the forge is no longer seen. The groaning of the huge water wheel, the creaking, creaking of the ore-laden wagons, and the ring of the hammer are no longer heard. The old-fashioned leader belows is forgotten. The pungent smell and smoke of the charcoal fires no longer hover over these hills. The shout and cry of the carters are stilled. The forge is in the dust. But yonder little stream meanders on through these pleasant valleys, amid fertile fields, in bucolic murmurings, as it did long before the white man harnessed its falls, dammed its ripples and made it work—all unmindful of what man could do to it—save here and there a degenerate and dilapidated saw or grist mill ekes out a precarious existence—a sad commentary on the glories that were.

But lo! The waters of this stream gathering with the waters of many others into the mighty Susquehanna are again harnessed by man at Holtwood, and its energy, transformed into "white coal," are sent back in the form of electricity to illumine this quiet valley and ease the burden of man and beast.

So with the spirit and genius of Windsor. It, too, like the little stream, has gone forth to broader fields. The children who were born here, and their children and children's children have been going to and fro in the far places of the world, doing good, spreading the culture, refinement and knowledge which were cradled here, and in ever-widening circles are found in business, in the pulpit, and class room, in art, literature, science, in the professions and in the home.

And now for half a century the old mansion slept, quiescent, tenderly sheltered by the ancient trees which stood guard o'er its portals whispering in their soughing to one another and to the babbling brook beyond, the memories, the stories, the traditions of bygone days.

For half a century Windsor awaited the coming of its present Mistress, who with artistic feeling and respect for her forebears and the early history of her State rehabilitated it, rescued it from its decrepitude and revivified its old bones. The genius of the place circumnavigated the globe, and gathering into its bosom the best of distant lands and strange civilizations, with affection and discriminating appreciation has regenerated itself and added a new lustre and brilliancy to the romance and story of the past. Once again its hospitable doors swing open wide to all the world of worth and honor, and on this day its present Mistress deeply appreciates the personal cordiality of the Pilgrims of the Berks County Historical Society.

Dear Old Windsor Forges—like old Buddha, incarnation of the past whose enigmatic visage, sculptured by your present Mistress, greets your guests by your door—may your story, too, go on and on and be unravelled from age to age in newer generations, worthy descendants of the old pioneers who builded here. May your reincarnated spirit and genius, like that of yonder brook transformed into electricity for man's enjoyment and profit, be as powerful for the elevating and constructive influences of human kind.

Bibliography Sources

1. Lodge and Pickens. *Appleton's Cyclopedia of American Art.* Ed. Wilson and Fiske. Vol. 4., D. Appleton and Co., 1888.

2. Meginnes, J. John Co. *Biographical Annals of Lancaster County,* Illustrated, Pub. J. H. Beers and Co, 1903.

3. *Gale Biographical Index Series #1.* Biography and Geneology Master, Vol. 2-H-O. Index 1986-90. Barbara McNeil, Ed., Gale Research Inc., Detroit. New York.

4. Weiman, Jeanne Madeline. *The Fair Women,* The story of the Woman's Building, World's Columbia Exposition, Chicago, IL. 1893. Pub. Academy, Chicago, IL. 1981.

5. Archives, *Nevin File.* Santee Chapel, United Church of Christ Archives, Lancaster, PA.

6. Ellis, Franklin and Evans, Samuel. *History of Lancaster County, Biographical Sketches.* Pub. Everts and Peck, 1883.

7. *Biographical Annals of Lancaster County, Pennsylvania.* Vol. 1, Pub. Reprint Co., Spartansburg, SC, 1985.

8. Sayre, Francis Bowes. *Glad Adventure.* Autobiography. The MacMillan Co., New York, 1957.

9. Sayre, Robert H. Sayre, President of Southern Pennsylvania Railroad. *Personal Diaries.* Archives. Hugh Moore Park and Canal Museum, Easton, PA.

10. *The Loan Show Book.* First art show in the Woolworth Building with the Iris Club and Lancaster County Historical Society, 1912.

11. Appel, Theodore. *Life and Work of John Williamson Nevin.* Copyright, Intelligencer Printing, 1889.

12. Simpson, Robert. *The Rambler.* Churchtown Historical Society. Churchtown, PA.

13. McElroy, Janice, ed. *Dictionary of Artists in America,* Lancaster Public Library, 1915-1983.

14. Fielding, Mantle. *Dictionary of American Painters, Sculptors and Engravers.* Modern Books and Crafts, Inc., 1926.

15. *Nevin File.* Lancaster County Historical Society. Lancaster, PA.

16. *Caernarvon File.* Lancaster County Historical Society, Lancaster, PA.

17. Rebman, Earl F. *Outline of History,* 1710-1980.

18. *Art in the Woman's Pavilion.* 1876 Exposition in Philadelphia.

19. Nicolai, Jr., Civosky. *Nineteenth Century American Women Neo-classical Sculptors.* Vassar College Art Gallery, 1972.

20. Leslie, Frank. *Illustrated Historical Register of the Centennial Exposition.* Frank Leslie Publishing House, 1878.

21. Ingram, J. S. *The Centennial Exposition.* Hubbard Bros., Philadelphia, PA. N. D. Thompson and Co., St. Louis, MO, 1876.

22. Mast and Simpson. *The Annals of Conestoga Valley.* Mennonite Pub. House, Scottsdale, PA, 1942.

23. McElroy, Janice. *Pennsylvania Women in History, Our Hidden Heritage,* 1983.

24. Archambault, A Margaretta. *A Guide of Art, Architecture and Historic Interests in Pennsylvania.* John C. Winston, Philadelphia, PA, 1924.

25. *Programme Notes and Minutes.* Lancaster County Historical Society, Lancaster, PA.

Vol. 1   1896-97, p. 377
              Poem p. 381, 1897, June 4

Vol. 13   The Automobile Party, p. 195

Vol. 15 1911, p. 271

Vol. 16 1912, Loan Exhibition
              Bust of Woodrow Wilson, p. 71
              Bust of Catherine Carmichael, 1774-1856
              Busts and Woodcarvings, p. 108

Vol. 17 Society Annual Outing to Elizabeth Furnace, July 11, 1913

Vol. 18 Robert Jenkins, Congress 1807-1811

Vol. 19 1915-16 meetings

Vol. 21 1917 meeting in Iris Club Rooms, p. 49

Vol. 22 Muhlenberg Statue 1918, p. 147

Vol. 24 Windsor Forge Fords of Conestoga River, 1920

Vol. 29 Windsor Forges

Vol. 39 Churchtown, 1935, p. 67

Vol. 75 Painting Dr. John Stahr, 1971, p. 34

Vol. 80 Caernarvon Place, 1976, p. 99

Vol. XIX Newspaper Article. Lancaster County Historical Society, p. 200-206

Vol. 22 P. 156; 165-166; 295. Ref. AAA, Fielding; Paine; Becker; Theime; Vassar; Weiman.

28. *Biographical Annals of Lancaster County.* Illustrated. Fackenthal Library, Franklin and Marshall College. Pub. J. H. Beers and Co., 1903.

29. The Kittochtinny Historical Society, Franklin County, PA. *Papers read before the Society,* Vol. XIV. 1956, October to April, 1963.

30. *Old Mercersburg.* By Womens Club of Mercersburg, PA, 1949.

31. Heckscher, August. *Woodrow Wilson.* Collier Books, MacMillan Pub. Co., New York, 1991.

32. White, George M. *Copy of Pennsylvania Art Commission report to Governor Hartranft and personal notes from Blanche Nevin.* Architect of the Capitol, 1793. Washington DC, Statuary Hall.

33. Klein, H. M. J. *Lancaster's Golden Century.* 1821-1921 to commemorate one hundred years of the house of Hager, April 1921. Published by Hager and Brothers, Wickersham Printing Company, Lancaster, PA, 1921.

34. The New York Historical Society. 170 Central Park West, New York, New York, 10094-5194. *The New York Times,* April 22,1925. Obituary for Blanche Nevin.

35. Opitz, Glenn B., ed. *Dictionary of American Painters, Sculptors and Engravers.* Poughkeepsie, NY. Apollo, 1986.

36. The Historical Society of Pennsylvania, Philadelphia. *Buchanan File.*

37. Vassar and Weiman. Fielding, Paine, Thieme, Becker. Ref. AAA V. 22 obit. , pp. 156, 165-66, 295.

38. Lancaster Mennonite Historical Society Library.

39. History of Lancaster County, Vol. 2, Ellis and Evans.

40. Hugh Moore Park Museum Inc. Archives. Easton, PA. Diaries

of Robert Sayre, 1891-1903.

41. Diffenderfer, Frank Reid, Litt. D. *A History of The Farmers Bank of Lancaster, The Farmers National Bank and The Farmers Trust Company of Lancaster, 1810-1910*. Pub. Farmers Trust Co. of Lancaster, Lancaster, PA, 1910.

42. Nevin, Blanche. *Souvenir of the Pilgramage of The Historical Society of Berks County to Windsor Forges, 1742*. Caernarvon Township, Lancaster County, Pennsylvania. September 2, 1921. Lancaster County.

43. Nevin, Blanche. *Great-Grandma's Looking Glass,* a poem with illustrations by Annis Dunbar Jenkins. (These are miniature silhouettes) Pub. Robert Grier Cooke, Inc., NY MDCCCCV, (1905) Millersville University Special Collection, 811.5N 416, Ganser Library, Millersville, PA.

44. Colonial Dames. *Forges and Furnaces of the Province of Pennsylvania,* 1914, p. 101.

45. Muhlenberg, Henry A. *The Life of Major General Peter Muhlenberg of the Revolutionary Army*. Carey and Hart, Philadelphia 1849. LCHS.

46. Mann, William. *Life and Times of Henry Melchior Muhlenberg*. G. W. Frederick, Philadelphia, 1888.

47. Heitman, Francis B., addenda Kelly Robert. *Continental Army*. 1914, Reprinted Geneological Pub. Co. Inc., Baltimore 1967, 1973, 1982, ISBO 8063-0176-6, LCCCN 67-22180.

48. Nevin, David Robert. *Continental Sketches of Distinguished Pennsylvanians*. Lancaster County Historical society, 923.2 N 526, 1875.

49. Heisey, M. Luther. *William Wilberforce Nevin, "The Gallant 79th." 1836-99*, Lancaster County Historical Society, 1962, 974.9 L 245.

50. Whittier, John Greenleaf. *The Complete Writings of John Greenleaf Whittier,* Amesbury Edition, Vol. 1 of Seven Volumes. AMS Press, New York, 1894, Reprinted 1969. 811.36 W618C, V. 1. Millersville University, Ganser Library.

51. Hocker, Edward W. *The Fighting Parson of the American Revolution,* A Biography of General Peter Muhlenberg, Lutheran Clergyman, Military Chieftain, and Political Leader. Published by author, Philadelphia, PA, 1936.

52. Blanche Nevin file, The Historical Society of Pennsylvania.

53. Pennypacker, Samuel Whitaker, Gov. 1903-1907. *The Autobiography of a Pennsylvanian.* The John C. Winston Co., Philadelphia, 1918.

54. Jenkins, Howard M., ed. *Pennsylvania; Colonial and Federal, A History 1608-1903.* The Pennsylvania Historical Publishing Association. Vol. 1, 1903.

55. FDR Library Elderhostel, September 1995, Hyde Park, NY Library, Museum and Archives at Springwood.

56. Rubenstein, Charlotte S. *American Women Sculptors: A History of Women Working in Three Dimensions.* Boston, MA. Hall and Co, 1990.

57. Hastings, Alice, *In Preparation for '76, Our Heritage.* Churchtown Historical Society Files; Article in "The Penny Saver," February 19, 1975.

58. Klimuska, Ed. The *Lancaster New Era,* staff writer. *Blanche*

Nevin: Artist, Sculptress, Free Spirit. Lancaster New Era, Tuesday, August 30, 1988.

59. Leaman, Rev. John, MD. *Tribute to the Memory of Mrs. Catherine M. Jenkins of Windsor* Place, Joseph M. Wilson, 27 S. Tenth Street, Philadelphia, PA, 1857.

60. Rothman Gallery, Steinman Building, Franklin and Marshall College. *Nevin file.* Letter from Robert Nevin.

61. Lancaster County Courthouse Archives.

62. Falk, Peter Hastings. *The Annual Exhibition Record of the Pennsylvania Academy of the Fine Arts.* 1876-1913. Sound View Press, 1989.

63. Weiler, John R., 325 Carver Drive., Bethlehem, PA. *Monograph, The Express Times,* Easton, PA, 8/26/93.

64. Schindler, Faith Sayre, grand-niece of Blanche Nevin. Family materials.